Genetic Engineering

By Eve and Albert Stwertka

Franklin Watts · A GROLIER COMPANY · An Impact Book
New York | London | Toronto | Sydney | 1982

Our very special thanks go to

Cold Spring Harbor Laboratory
where Dr. William Topp
was our host and guide;

to Dr. Ernest Lieber and staff of
the Department of Human Genetics,
Lond Island Jewish–Hillside Hospital,
who gave us a generous share of
their time and experience;

and to Jackson Laboratory,
Bar Harbor, Maine, where we
obtained pictures and diagrams and
had an informative talk with
Dr. Edward Birkenmeier.

We are also grateful to
New England Biolabs and
Bethesda Research Laboratories
for their catalogs.

Diagrams courtesy of Vantage Art, Inc.

Photographs courtesy of
Carolina Biological Supply Company:
pp. 59, 60.

Library of Congress Cataloging in Publication Data

Stwertka, Eve.
Genetic engineering.

(An Impact book)
Bibliography: p.
Includes index.
Summary: Discusses recombinant DNA techniques;
the application of this technology, including
amniocentesis, genetic counseling, and test-tube parenthood;
and the controversy surrounding these new discoveries.
1. Genetic engineering—Juvenile literature.
[1. Genetic engineering] I. Stwertka, Albert.
II. Title.
QH442.S78   575.2   82-7059
ISBN 0-531-04486-6   AACR2

Contents

Genetic
Engineering

1

The New Biology

In 1962, three young scientists—Francis Crick, James Watson, and Maurice Wilkins—received the Nobel Prize for discovering the structure of DNA, or deoxyribonucleic acid. DNA is the substance that carries the genetic information of living matter. It is not only basic to every growing cell of the human body, it determines the composition of all forms of life, from the largest plants and animals to most of the tiniest viruses. Everything that lives is programmed to take on a definite size, shape, and mode of existence all its own. This program is dictated by the code within the DNA of each organism.

The new discovery opened the field of molecular biology, which is an umbrella term for the branch of science dealing with the smallest structures of living matter. Within this field, experimentation with DNA by snipping, adding, or exchanging parts, is usually called recombinant DNA research. The technological offspring of recombinant DNA research is genetic engineering. This is the practical application of discoveries to turn them into useful and commercially profitable ventures. Such ventures range from medicine and pharmacology to agriculture, food processing, mining, and chemical manufacture. Scientists are also using genetic engineering techniques to investigate the basic causes of hereditary disorders and of illnesses such as cancer.

INSIDE A
MOLECULAR BIOLOGY LAB

The Cold Spring Harbor Laboratory complex of Long Island, New York, is one of many institutions that are equipped to do research with DNA. Just now, for example, the work of James Laboratory, the Tumor Virus Division of the complex, is focused on viruses that cause breast tumors in rats. One of the lab's projects is to study how these viruses change the cells they infect and how the changes relate to the growth of cancerous tumors.

It is known that specific viruses produce breast tumors in live rats. To find out exactly how this happens, the researchers induce small changes in the DNA of the viruses. They then allow the viruses to attack mammalian cells, to see how these will be affected. The cells are not observed in the live animals but *in vitro*, that is, in the controlled environment of laboratory glassware.

A visitor walking through the corridors of James Lab sees flasks of rose-colored liquid shelved in glass cabinets. They contain human cells suspended in a nutrient solution of amino acids and vitamins. In every room, researchers lean over laboratory benches, intent on their tasks.

In a black-walled cubicle, a young woman in a lab coat concentrates on a high-powered microscope in front of her. She is microinjecting pieces of DNA into a single mammalian cell. The tip of the pipette she must insert into the cell nucleus has an inner diameter of .5 micrometers, or five ten-thousandths of a millimeter (1 mm = 0.039 in).

Rows of warming cabinets hold a thick soup of cell-growing material kept moving by automatic stirrers. Outside the Cold Room, which looks very much like a butcher's refrigerator, stand blue, thick-necked, knee-high vacuum bottles called Dewar flasks. Nearby are gleaming steel vats of liquid nitrogen. Assorted cells that have been carefully frozen are stored in these vats, sometimes for as long as a decade.

In a corner of each lab section, a small lead-shielded area is set aside to contain materials made radioactive for observation. A darkroom is available for developing X-ray and other film. Central to the lab is a sterilizer for laboratory garments and equipment. It is set in the wall like a huge laundry dryer.

The equipment molecular biologists use is simple and inexpensive compared to that needed by other branches of science. Cold Spring Harbor owns three electron microscopes. Aside from this costly research apparatus, the rest is standard gear in any biological laboratory.

James Lab is not a high-risk facility. According to government regulatory standards, experiments are classified by the levels of physical containment that are required. These levels range from P1 (low risk) to P4 (high risk). James is rated P2.

Very few facilities in the United States are engaged in P4-level research. One of them is Plum Island, the Department of Agriculture's Animal Disease Center, offshore in Long Island Sound. James Lab does have a small P3 room at the back of the building. Access is restricted to the few people who work there. On entering they put on protective gowns. On leaving, they drop these on the ground, to be sterilized. In the entry there is a negative air curtain, a space closed off by two doors, in which the air pressure is kept slightly lower than outside. This causes air to move in rather than out and prevents bacteria from being carried off limits.

In the rest of the laboratory, P2 regulations are strictly observed. Eating and drinking are not permitted and lab coats must be worn.

The scientists carry out many of their manipulations at hooded benches. While their hands reach under the curved glass hood, they can look through the transparent surface that shields them from inhaling any microorganisms. At the same time, the hood protects the microorganisms from contamination.

Research at this lab requires strictly controlled conditions. To prevent the accidental meeting of cultured viruses and cultured cells, the two are isolated on separate floors. Cells grow upstairs, viruses downstairs. Upstairs, containment hoods are mainly important in keeping foreign organisms out, while downstairs the hoods are needed to keep the viruses in. When the cells on the upper floor are ready, a researcher brings them down a flight to be infected under supervision.

MILESTONES IN DNA RESEARCH

Molecular biology and genetic engineering are fields of brilliant possibilities. Both have grown rapidly within a few decades. Because the equipment needed is comparatively simple, recombinant DNA laboratories have been installed in most universities and hospitals. Similar labs form part of industrial plants and exist as independent commercial enterprises.

What makes Cold Spring Harbor special, however, is, among other things, that it began its latest phase of expansion under James D. Watson, its director since 1977. Dr. Watson, you will remember, was a member of the team that discovered the DNA structure in 1953, resulting in a Nobel Prize in 1962.

The Model of the DNA Molecule

Many brilliant predecessors and contemporaries had provided the ideas and research data on which the team's discovery was founded. But the final breakthrough came after Crick and Watson used a new and seemingly playful approach to the problem. Instead of relying entirely on chemical analysis and X-ray observation, they tried making a large model of the DNA molecule. With sheet metal cutouts and wire they attempted to work out a structure that would accommodate all the chemical elements of which DNA was known to be composed.

After several false starts, they suddenly realized that DNA must consist of not one, but *two* long, thin molecules twisted about each other in the form of a double helix, very much like a ladder turned into a circular staircase. Along

■4■

this structure, chemical groups called bases are arranged in pairs to form the rungs of the ladder. Although there are only four bases, they can be ordered in many different sequences. In fact, the number of possible arrangements is astronomical, since any base can be repeated any number of times. These sequences spell out the particular code for the growth and reproduction of each living cell and organism.

Heredity, Genes, and Nuclein

For hundreds of years, people seldom asked why elephants always give birth to more elephants and not to giraffes or other animals. The fact that children look like their parents was taken for granted.

It was known, of course, that by careful breeding one could change the characteristics of offspring. One could select horses with particularly long legs, allow them to mate, and pick only the longest-legged foals for mating again. In this way, new generations of racehorses might be created, looking very different from their early ancestors. Selective breeding had long been practiced to give farmers cows that produced more milk or hogs that were meaty rather than fatty. Gardeners, too, had been aware for centuries that crossbreeding certain plants produced new forms.

Guesswork was the basis of most of these experiments until 1865. In that year, an Austrian monk, Gregor Mendel, published the results of his careful five-year study of heredity in garden peas. Little regarded at the time, his findings were rediscovered thirty-five years later, when three European biologists, working independently, arrived at the same results. By using statistical methods, these scientists were able to discern the basic laws that govern inheritance of traits. The science of genetics was born.

Mendel had no way of knowing what elements within the pea plant contained the signals of heredity. He simply thought of them as "inheritance factors." Later, these factors came to be called genes. Today we know that each gene is a long strand of DNA made up of subunits named nucleotides, whose number may reach into the thousands.

Only four years after Mendel's publication, an apparently unrelated discovery was made in Switzerland. A young chemist named Friedrich Miescher was experimenting with white blood cells which he obtained from the pus on used hospital bandages. It was Miescher's uncle, the well-known anatomist Wilhelm His, who had turned the young chemist's attention to the study of living tissue. Wilhelm His had a hunch that the secrets of biology would ultimately be solved by chemical analysis. In the process of his work with white blood cells, Miescher isolated a substance he called nuclein. Nuclein was, in fact, a combination of proteins and DNA. Here was the beginning of biochemistry as a new branch of specialization.

Neither Friedrich Miescher nor his contemporaries understood just how nuclein functioned in the cell. They suspected that it exerted some influence on hereditary processes; but the crucial insight was not won until 1944, when Oswald Avery, an American scientist, proved that DNA is, in fact, the basic hereditary substance.

Phage Research
In 1945 a group of biologists began concentrated research on bacteriophages, minute viruses that invade and infect only bacteria. These organisms had been observed and studied as early as 1915 by the French biologist Felix d'Hérelle, who also named them. (The word is based on a Greek root and means "bacteria-eaters.")

Phage, as they are commonly called, are formations of such relative simplicity that they hover on the margin between lifeless chemical molecules and live organisms. As we shall see, phage research was an important step toward discovering the genetic role of DNA and thus ushering in what later came to be called the new biology. (See *Viruses*, pages 10–11.)

The "Phage Group" was led by Max Delbrück of the University of California Institute of Technology and his associates Salvador Luria and Alfred Hershey.

A New Way to Study Biology

A slender volume published in 1944 focused the scientific community's attention on an ancient, basic question. *What Is Life?* was the book's title. The author was Erwin Schrödinger, a physicist of great renown. He suggested that the time had come for physicists, with their mathematical methods, to join biologists and chemists in the study of life. By examining the three-dimensional structures of biological molecules, physical chemistry would help unlock the innermost secrets of the living cell.

Francis Crick was one of several physicists whose interest was thus drawn to molecular biology. Some years later, summing up changes that had occurred in the field, Crick wrote: "The ultimate aim of the modern movement in biology is in fact to explain all biology in terms of physics and chemistry."

Genetic Engineering Technology

As soon as the structure of DNA was understood, new developments followed. The stuff of heredity could now be manipulated and used to human advantage. In the early 1970s, researchers developed techniques for cleaving, or splitting, the DNA molecule by means of enzymes. Enzymes are proteins originating in living cells, that act as catalysts to produce complex changes in other organic substances. This is their role, for example, in the process of digesting food. After cleaving the DNA molecule, researchers could snip out certain parts and splice these to the DNA of other cells or viruses. The result was called recombinant DNA. Once developed, the procedures for constructing recombinant DNA turned out to be amazingly simple to perform. Now a cell could be altered to give and receive a new message. A bacterium could be programmed, for example, to produce a hormone or enzyme quite foreign to its original nature. Thus, bacterial colonies could be used almost like farms to produce various biological substances.

The first products of bio-engineering have been pharmaceuticals such as insulin, the essential hormone for diabetic patients, and interferon, an antiviral agent thought to confer disease resistance. Other innovations are in the making. In the future, shortages of food may be eased by genetically engineered proteins. Self-fertilizing grain varieties may bring a second Green Revolution. Microorganisms may be used to convert waste materials into plastics and fuels. In medicine, researchers are applying gene splicing to the study of cancer and birth defects, hoping to discover what causes these diseases and how they can be prevented or cured.

DECODING MESSAGES

A basic task for molecular biologists is to determine the number and location of DNA subunits in all forms of life, from microbes to humans. Surprisingly, this gene-mapping task is already complete for several microorganisms. One of them is that ancient crippler and threat to human life, the polio virus. Knowing the 7,740 chemical subunits of the polio virus's eight genes enables scientists to make the virus artificially, from laboratory chemicals. It also enables them to redesign it in a harmless form that will still make an effective vaccine.

In humans, though, gene mapping is far more difficult. Some three billion DNA subunits are estimated to make up the forty-six human chromosomes—the threadlike structures in each cell nucleus which carry the genes. At the present rate of decoding it would take several hundred years to do the job. Yet, genetic engineering techniques may take another amazing leap forward to help accomplish the task sooner than expected.

Because genetic engineering promises revolutionary improvements on so many fronts, it has developed at an explosive rate, with a subsidiary technology all its own to serve it. Automated equipment now cleaves and recombines segments of DNA, while other kinds of apparatus automatically count cells or analyze the sequence of amino acids in a protein sample. Such tools speed up the process of gaining insight into the secrets of the gene.

2
The Code of the Double Helix

In searching for the roots of heredity, modern biologists looked more and more deeply into the basic building blocks of life. The discovery that DNA, the molecule of heredity, is structured in the form of a double helix at last opened up a fundamental area of investigation: it allowed scientists to penetrate to the molecular level of the genetic puzzle.

Biologists had long known about the role of the chromosomes in determining heredity. Chromosomes are contained in all cells. The name "chromosome," meaning "colored body," dates back about a hundred years to the time when scientists first became curious about these little threads which showed up in dye-stained cell material under the microscope.

It is on the chromosomes that genes—the controllers of heredity—are arranged in rows. The genes, in turn, are made of DNA, deoxyribonucleic acid. The coded information carried in these molecules of DNA is used by the cells to produce the proteins, the most essential organic substances of living tissue.

Organisms as different as bacteria, plants, and humans have common features at the molecular level. They use the same building blocks to construct protein. The flow of genetic information from DNA to protein is essentially the same in all species.

THE EVIDENCE

The Transformation Principle
It was in the 1940s that Oswald T. Avery and his associates at the Rockefeller Institute showed that the hereditary properties of a harmless strain of pneumonia bacteria could be altered by the addition of foreign DNA from another bacterial strain. Avery took two strains of pneumonia bacteria—one virulent and one benign. When he isolated DNA from the virulent strain and added this nucleic acid to the benign strain, the latter became virulent too. Avery therefore called nucleic acid the fundamental unit of a *transformation principle*.

At first, many of Avery's colleagues were perplexed and hesitated to accept the implications of the seemingly magical DNA-induced transformation of benign bacteria into virulent bacteria. Nevertheless, Avery's experiment conclusively established DNA as the carrier of genetic information.

The Role of Viruses
Further evidence for the genetic role of DNA came from studies of bacteriophages, viruses that infect and multiply in bacteria.

We usually think of viruses as causative agents of certain diseases such as influenza and polio. The essential feature of viruses, however, is that they are dormant outside a living cell but multiply to form duplicate copies of themselves when they have infected a cell. They take over the chemical and energy-producing machinery of the cell to make all the vital biological molecules needed for their own reproduction.

Viruses consist of a core of either DNA or RNA enclosed within a protective protein coat which allows the virus to be transported from cell to cell. It was suggested in 1951 that a phage acts like a hypodermic needle. When a phage encounters a bacterium, an enzyme in the tail of the phage creates a hole in the cell wall of the bacterium through which the DNA of the virus flows into the cell. The viral DNA, carrying the hereditary information for repro-duction of the virus, makes some one hundred copies of itself. Eventually, the host cell bursts, or lyses, and the new viruses are released into the environment. The important principle demonstrated in these early phage experiments was that the viral DNA served as a template—a model or pattern—in the host cell, for the formation of other phage.

THE DOUBLE HELIX

Although they did not know its precise structure, chemists working with DNA had known for ten years or more that it was a very long molecule made up of repeating units of a five-carbon sugar called deoxyribose linked together by phosphate groups. Attached at regular intervals to the sug-ar molecules in the backbone of the long chain were chem-ical groups, called bases. There were always the same four standard bases: adenine (A), thymine (T), guanine (G), and cytosine (C). The sugar molecule, with its attached base and phosphate coupler, was named a nucleotide. They knew that the nucleotide units were linked one to the other in a long polynucleotide chain to form a thin threadlike substance. The sugar-phosphate backbone was constant throughout the DNA, but the sequence of bases they knew to be variable.

Then, in 1953, James Watson and Francis Crick, using X-ray diffraction photographs of DNA fibers and the new-ly developed theoretical insights into the nature of the chemical bond, deduced the now famous double-helix structure for DNA. As we have seen, Watson and Crick constructed a three-dimensional model showing DNA to be a *double* molecule with one polynucleotide chain coiled

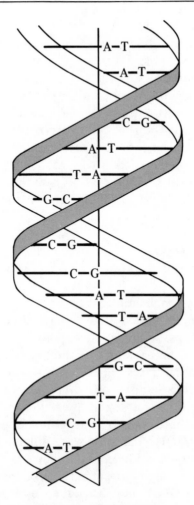

The DNA double helix.

The DNA molecule is a double helix composed of two strands. The sugar–phosphate backbones twist around the outside, with the paired bases on the inside serving to hold the chains together. Adenine (A) pairs with Thymine (T); Guanine (G) pairs with Cytosine (C).

around the other in the form of a helix. Crick and Watson proposed that the genetic information carried by each strand was encoded in the particular sequence of its bases.

The bases attached to the chains are on the inside of the helix and fit together very precisely. In order to fit, however, the bases on the two chains are always paired in exactly the same fashion. This was the discovery of Watson and Crick. Adenine always pairs with thymine, and guanine always pairs with cytosine. The paired bases, adenine and thymine for example, are called complementary bases. The exact pairing of complementary bases happens not only because of the physical restraints of fitting inside the helical coil, like the rungs of a ladder, but also because the electrical forces, called hydrogen bonds, between complementary base pairs act as the couplers that bind the two strands together.

The DNA model immediately made it obvious that knowing the sequence of bases on one strand would enable one to predict the complementary sequence on the other strand.

Semiconservative Replication
A month after their original paper on the structure of DNA, Watson and Crick presented a model for DNA replication. Their idea was that if the two chains were to unwind and separate, each chain would act as a template or pattern for the construction of its complementary chain. The idea of complementarity was often compared to a lock and key: given a lock, one can always manufacture a key to fit it; or given the key, one could construct a lock that would fit the key. (See diagram, page 14.)

A critical feature of this new model was that the sequence of base pairs in the original double helix was exactly duplicated in the "daughter." Each new daughter double helix that was formed would have one strand from its parent and one newly synthesized strand that was exact-

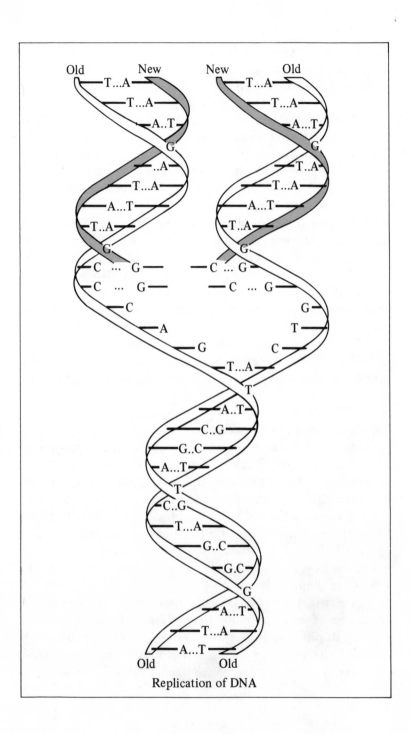

Replication of DNA

ly complementary. Biologists call this form of replication, where one strand of the double helix is always derived from a previously existing double helix, semiconservative replication.

DNA and Genes

Genes are portions of DNA. DNA molecules are very long and carry the information of many genes. The DNA of a bacteriophage, for example, is about 166,000 bases long, while that of a human is 2,900,000,000 bases long. Since the average size of a mammalian gene has been estimated from about 5,000 bases to 100,000 bases long, the number of genes carried on a single human DNA strand is enormous. If all the DNA in a human cell were stretched to its full length, it would be an incredible 1 meter (3 ft) long.

Many viral DNA molecules are circular, that is, the two ends are joined together to form a ring. For compactness, this ring can be twisted or supercoiled along one of its diameters. Supercoiling is similar to holding a rubber band in two hands and twisting the two ends in opposite directions. Besides being supercoiled, the DNA may also be wound around certain DNA-associated proteins called histones, which act as cores, or spools. The need for packaging DNA in compact form is obvious when one considers that the DNA must fit into cells thousands of times smaller in length. Some DNA can assume both a linear and a circular form. The DNA of some viruses, for example, is linear while it is contained within the viral protein, but becomes circular when injected into a host cell.

DNA Replication

The discovery of the double helix served to stimulate very rapid progress in molecular genetics. It was soon established that the two strands of DNA do not have to unwind completely for replication to begin. The replication of DNA always begins at a unique spot called the replication fork. At this site, as the DNA begins to unwind, manufacture of new DNA immediately begins.

What triggers the replication of DNA? Scientists have recently discovered an important clue in *E. coli* (*Escherichia coli*), the harmless bacteria that colonize the human intestine. Working with *E. coli* they discovered that a group of enzymes activates a small coded segment of DNA called the origin of replication. (In *E. coli* this segment is only 245 base units long, out of a total of four million.)

The actual construction of a new strand of DNA during replication is carried out by a group of enzymes called DNA polymerase and DNA ligase. Working together, they position the proper nucleotides onto the template and supply the energy to join them together and form a chain. The enzymes have an editing function as well, correcting errors of duplication that inevitably occur. In effect, the DNA polymerase examines the result of each addition to the chain before proceeding to the next. If an error is found, it removes the mismatched nucleotide. DNA ligase also has the ability to repair "nicks" in the DNA sugar phosphate backbone.

Many other proteins contribute to the complex replication process to assure its accuracy. High replication fidelity is necessary since even a few mismatched nucleotides might cause a mutation resulting in a nonfunctioning gene. The error rate has been estimated to be only one per ten million base pairs copied.

RNA

Messenger RNA and Transcription

In cells that contain a nucleus, almost all the DNA is found in the chromosomes of the nucleus. But the manufacture, or synthesis, of protein occurs outside the nucleus, in the body of the cell. How then is the information in the DNA molecule used to make the proteins that are vital to the life of the cell? The answer is in an intermediate molecule that carries the DNA instructions out of the nucleus.

The intermediate molecule that serves as "secondary blueprint" for protein synthesis is RNA, ribonucleic acid.

RNA is synthesized in the nucleus, according to instructions encoded in the DNA. This process is called transcription. Because this RNA then moves out into the body of the cell carrying its "message" to the ribosomes, where the proteins are made, it is called messenger RNA, mRNA. Ribosomes are able to "read" the genetic messages carried by the mRNA and to assemble accurately any kind of protein molecule. This process is called translation.

The flow of genetic information can be diagramed as follows:

$$DNA \longrightarrow RNA \longrightarrow Protein$$

$$transcription \longrightarrow translation$$

The Structure of RNA

Like DNA, RNA is a long threadlike molecule consisting of a sequence of four different nucleotides joined together by chemical bonds. RNA, however, is distinguished from DNA by differences in its chemical groups. The first difference is that the sugar unit in the molecule's backbone is ribose, from which RNA gets its name, rather than deoxyribose, as in DNA. The second is that in RNA the base uracil is substituted for thymine. The differences are rather slight. Uracil, like thymine, is complementary to adenine and can form base pairs with it. Finally, with only a few exceptions in viruses, RNA is single-stranded.

Forms of RNA

Cells actually contain three different kinds of RNA: messenger RNA (mRNA), transfer RNA (tRNA), and ribosomal RNA (rRNA). As we have seen, the mRNA carries instructions for the making of proteins to the cellular protein factory, the ribosomes. The ribosomes themselves, however, are largely made up of a form of RNA called ribosomal RNA. Although rRNA makes up the largest fraction of RNA in the cell, some eighty percent, its role in protein synthesis is still not known. Yet another form of

RNA, transfer RNA, collects the raw material or "building blocks," as we noted earlier, that will make up the protein, the chemical groups called amino acids, and "transfers" them to the ribosomes.

Proteins

Proteins play a crucial role in almost all biological processes. These vital substances, which comprise more than half the solid substance in the tissue of the human body, are constructed from just twenty kinds of building blocks called amino acids. All proteins in all species are made up of different combinations of these twenty amino acids. The differences between proteins depend on which amino acids are used and how they are arranged and sequenced. There is evidence that this "alphabet" of proteins is at least two billion years old.

The first scientist to decipher accurately the structure of a protein was Frederick Sanger. His chemical formula for the amino acid sequence of insulin, a protein hormone, won him the Nobel Prize in 1958. It was a momentous achievement because it showed for the first time that a protein has a precisely defined amino acid sequence.

Proteins, like DNA molecules, can be very large. The insulin molecule, for example, contains 777 atoms. Some protein molecules are fifty to sixty times larger.

Each kind of protein has a unique amino acid sequence. The change of a single amino acid in a protein can cause it to malfunction and produce disease in the entire organism. Sickle cell anemia, for example, is caused by the substitution of just one amino acid for another in the hundreds of amino acids that make up hemoglobin in the blood.

THE GENETIC CODE

The amino acid sequences of proteins are genetically determined, and the genetic code is the relationship linking the sequence of bases in DNA or RNA to the sequence of amino acids in proteins. It allows us to translate the "four letter" (four bases) language of DNA into the "twenty letter" (twenty amino acids) language of protein.

Since there are only four bases in DNA or RNA but twenty amino acids in proteins, each amino acid must be specified by some combination of more than one base. Experimental evidence has established that a sequence of three bases stands for one amino acid. Such a triplet group is called a codon. The genetic message which dictates the amino acid sequences in proteins consists of consecutive triplets with no overlapping. Thus the sequence AAACCAGGCCUG of an RNA molecule is read as follows:

AAA	CCA	GGC	CUG
amino acid 1	amino acid 2	amino acid 3	amino acid 4

Taking the four bases, A, C, G, and U, in groups of three, one can form sixty-four distinct codons. (There are $4 \times 4 \times 4$ different possible triplet combinations.) All sixty-four codons have been deciphered. Sixty-one of them correspond to particular amino acids, and three, the triplets, UAG, UAA, and UGA, represent punctuation in the form of a signal to stop or terminate the synthesis. The genetic code is shown in the table on page 20.

Since there are only twenty amino acids, many of the acids are designated by more than one of the sixty-four available codons. Several codons, in other words, may stand for one amino acid. This built-in redundancy is thought to be important in minimizing the accidental changes that might occur in the base sequence. Changes such as the substitution of one base for another, or a base being left out of the sequence, are the major causes of mutations.

The genetic code represents a universal language. It is the same in plants, viruses, bacteria, and humans. There is strong evidence, furthermore, that it has remained the same through billions of years of evolution.

THE GENETIC CODE

AAU AAC } Asparagine

AAA AAG } Lysine

AGU AGC } Serine
AGA AGG } Arginine

AUU AUC AUA } Isoleucine
AUG — Methionine

ACU ACC ACA ACG } Threonine

GAU GAC } Aspartic acid

GAA GAG } Glutamic acid

GGU GGC GGA GGG } Glycine

GUU GUC GUA GUG } Valine

GCU GCC GCA GCG } Alanine

CAU CAC } Histidine

CAA CAG } Glutamine

CGU CGC CGA CGG } Arginine

CUU CUC CUA CUG } Leucine

CCU CCC CCA CCG } Proline

UAU UAC } Tyrosine

UAA UAG } Stop signals

UGU UGC } Cysteine
UGA — Stop signal
UGG — Tryptophan

UUU UUC } Phenylalanine
UUA UUG } Leucine

UCU UCC UCA UCG } Serine

Each amino acid is represented by one or more base-triplets, and each base-triplet stands for one specific amino acid.

The Code in Complex Cells

The DNA making up the genes of simple organisms such as bacteria consists of an unbroken stretch of codons, the universal alphabet of DNA. It came as a major surprise when it was discovered in 1977 that the genes of higher organisms such as animal cells have their coded sequences interrupted by sequences of noncoding bases. Much to scientists' astonishment, the series of codons for a particular protein was discontinuous, containing large segments of "nonsense" interrupting the real hereditary message. The surprise has been heightened by the further discovery that many of the intervening noncoding segments have persisted in some genes for hundreds of millions of years.

The coding sequences of these so-called split genes are called exons, for expressed regions, while the "nonsense" sequences are named introns. The gene for collagen, for example, the connective tissue material in all complex animals, contains fifty introns and fifty-one exons.

Another distinguishing feature of the DNA in complex cells is that the chromosome often contains sequences of bases that repeat themselves. Thirty percent of human DNA, for example, consists of short base sequences repeated at least twenty times.

The role played by the introns is still very much a mystery. It has been suggested that they might confer some important advantage in gene evolution.

Transfer RNA and Translation

The series of steps leading from the sequence of codon triplets on the mRNA to the final synthesis of proteins is complicated. It begins with amino acids, the building blocks of proteins, becoming attached to the relatively small transfer RNA (tRNA) molecules. The tRNA molecules are constructed in a specialized way so as to collect amino acids to be built into proteins. Each tRNA molecule collects one, and only one, kind of amino acid. There is an amino acid attachment site at one end of the molecule, and a loop called an anticodon loop at the other end. The anticodon

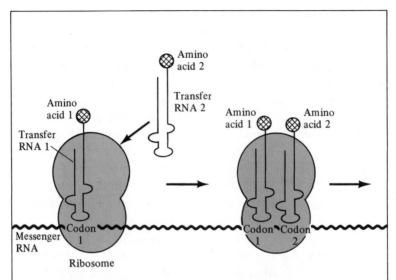

1. Here, tRNA 1, carrying amino acid 1, has bound itself to the first codon of mRNA to start protein synthesis, as tRNA 2 approaches.

2. Next, tRNA 2, carrying amino acid 2, positions itself on codon 2 of the mRNA.

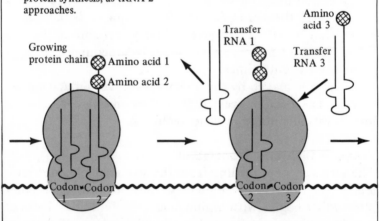

3. Amino acid 1 then displaces itself from its tRNA and binds to amino acid 2, starting the protein chain.

4. Now tRNA 1 is free of its charge and leaves. The next codon on the mRNA moves into position to be read by the incoming tRNA 3. Thus continues the sequence of building protein.

A ribosome moving along mRNA in the process of making protein.

loop is the recognition site that allows the tRNA, carrying its amino acid, to match the proper codon on a mRNA molecule. Recognition occurs by base pairing, since the bases on the anticodon are complementary to the bases on the mRNA. Similar to the pairing of bases on the DNA helix, A always pairs with U, and G always pairs with C.

The actual process of protein synthesis takes place on the ribosomes. A ribosome is a highly specialized structure made up of proteins and ribosomal RNA. The manufacture of proteins begins with the ribosome attaching itself to mRNA, and proceeds with the ribosome moving along the mRNA from codon to codon. Specific tRNA molecules carrying their attached amino acids are attracted to the matching codons on the mRNA template. Enzymes within the ribosome remove the amino acid groups from the tRNA and bind them together in the proper sequence to form the protein coded by the mRNA.

3

A Lesson in Gene Splicing

The power to take genetic material from one organism and insert it into another is a dramatic achievement in the history of science. It allows scientists to produce new combinations of entirely unrelated genes. Certain combinations of DNA made up in this way are often called chimeric DNA, after the mythical fire-breathing monster known as the Chimera. The Chimera had a lion's head, a goat's body, and a serpent's tail.

It is now possible to isolate a single gene from the thousands of genes of an animal cell and insert it into a bacterial chromosome. As the bacteria multiply they make millions of copies of the added gene and, in some cases, the protein coded by the gene. This process of allowing bacteria whose DNA has been altered to multiply and produce a large number of genetically identical copies is usually called cloning. A clone is a genetically identical cell descended from a single parent cell. Using cloning techniques, we can produce significant amounts of hormones such as insulin and human interferon.

Scientists are also introducing new combinations of genes into cells in an attempt to cure some of the diseases known to be caused by defective gene structure. By transferring a functioning gene into the cell, or correcting the mistake in the DNA, it is hoped that a cure for genetic illness will be found.

RECOMBINATION AND TRANSFORMATION

Even before the advent of modern recombinant DNA techniques, it was known that closely related species—those containing chromosomes with similar base sequences—could exchange segments of DNA. This exchange, known as homologous recombination, usually occurred during some mating process.

A procedure had also been developed for combining genetic information from organisms that were not closely related. The transfer of genes from one cell to another had been accomplished by bringing together cells whose outer cell walls had been removed by a suitable enzyme. These so-called protoplasts (cells without cell walls) would then fuse, forming a hybrid cell containing the chromosomes of both parent cells.

The most effective way of breaking down the natural barriers to recombination was the development of techniques that permitted scientists to insert foreign DNA directly into a new cell by a process known as transformation. The key to the success of these new techniques was the discovery of a form of DNA called a vector. A vector is a DNA molecule into which foreign DNA can be easily inserted, and which will then be efficiently taken up by the host cell. In order to show clearly that the vector has indeed been taken up by the host cell, it is important that the vector confer some property on the host cell that wasn't there before.

VECTORS: TOOLS FOR RECOMBINATION

Plasmids

The discovery of plasmids provided science with a useful vector for genetic recombination. Plasmids are small circular bits of DNA that float free in bacteria. These double-stranded DNA molecules exist outside the bacterial chromosome. Plasmids differ from the usual bacterial DNA in not being essential to the everyday metabolism of the cell. They vary in size, carrying as few as two genes or as many as two hundred. There are usually some two to thirty-five copies of a plasmid per cell, and they reproduce at about the same rate as the cell.

Considered an oddity at first, plasmids have now been found in virtually every bacterial species. Although most plasmids do not contribute to the usual hereditary information carried by a cell, they have been shown to increase the cell's resistance to certain toxic materials as well as to a variety of antibiotics. Some plasmids were found to carry information enabling bacteria to transfer genetic material to each other in a process, called conjugation, that resembles mating.

F Factor Plasmids and Conjugation

Nothing could have been more surprising than the discovery in the 1940s that there are "male" and "female" bacteria. Equally astonishing was the discovery of the existence of the mating process called conjugation. During conjugation, a special appendage called a sex pilus projects from the surface of the male bacteria and binds itself to certain sites on the female. DNA is transferred through the pilus from the male to the female.

The genes responsible for the formation of the sex pilus were found to be contained in a plasmid called the F factor (fertility factor). The so-called male bacterial cells contain the F factor.

Occasionally the F factor plasmid can become physically attached to the bacterial chromosome and become an integral part of it. When this happens, the entire chromosome is donated during mating.

R Factor Plasmids

This ability of plasmids to transfer genes between cells was demonstrated by a discovery made during an epidemic of bacterial dysentery that took place in Japan in 1959. A strain of *Shigella dysenteriae* bacteria was found to have become resistant to a whole host of antibiotics and therefore to be very difficult to treat. The genes responsible for conferring resistance were found to be linked together on a plasmid called an R factor (resistance factor) plasmid. This plasmid also contained genes similar to those of the F factor that enabled the R factor plasmid to be transmitted to other bacteria by conjugation. Resistance to antibiotics, apparently, was transferable. The clinical implications of this fact were rather frightening.

When R factor plasmids were first discovered, they commonly carried genes for one or two resistance traits. Today it is not uncommon to find a plasmid carrying genes for resistance to as many as ten different antibiotics. Analysis of this phenomenon revealed that the genes responsible for resistance to a single antibody were themselves small plasmids that lacked the ability to be transmitted by conjugation on their own. These individual r-genes (resistance genes) were highly mobile, however, and could easily insert themselves into more complex plasmids containing the transfer ability.

Lambda Phage

Another useful vector was the bacterial virus known as lambda. When DNA from a bacteriophage enters a bacterial cell, it usually takes over immediate control of the metabolism of the cell. Within about twenty minutes, several hundred new offspring viruses are produced, eventually bursting and killing the cell.

It was soon noticed that the behavior of lambda phage was strikingly different. After entering the cell, its DNA became integrated with the bacterial chromosome in the same fashion as the F factor plasmid. In this state most of the phage functions are dormant and it simply replicates as part of the host chromosome. It is stable in this form and can be transmitted through many generations without harming the cell. A variety of agents, including ultraviolet light, X rays, and certain chemicals, can "activate" the viral DNA, and cause it to become virulent again.

Lambda viruses have another interesting property. When they become detached from the host chromosome, the excision process is not always exact, and occasionally some of the host genes are carried away with the viral DNA. Reinfection of other bacteria with this modified lambda virus has the effect of an interchange of genes between the original host and the new cell. Like the F factor, then, the lambda virus can act as a vehicle to exchange genes.

Other viruses, such as the tumor virus SV40, have been discovered to act like lambda phage, and these too have become important tools in recombinant-DNA technique.

Selection of Vectors and Clones

Plasmids and lambda phage are the most frequently used vectors in the process of cloning. They are used to introduce foreign DNA into a bacterial cell. Both plasmids and lambda phage are easily introduced into a host bacterial cell by the process called transformation. The process essentially consists in mixing the vectors with the bacterial cells—*E. coli*, for example—whose membranes have been made extremely permeable by treatment with a calcium salt.

The resistance genes carried by plasmids make them sensitive indicators of which cells have taken up the vector. For example, plasmids containing r-genes for, let us say, three antibiotics, will usually have one of these genes inactivated by cleavage with restriction enzymes and the subsequent splicing of foreign DNA into the plasmid. Cells that have failed to take up the vector will be sensitive to all three antibiotics; cells containing the plasmid without the DNA insert will be resistant to all three; but cells that have taken up the vector will be resistant to two of the antibiotics.

Lambda phage has proven another excellent vector since large parts of its genome (the total sum of its genes) are not essential for infecting (entering) the bacterial host. The lambda DNA is cleaved with a restriction enzyme, and one of the resulting fragments—the essential one for viral replication—is spliced to a foreign strand of DNA. When this chimera is repackaged in its protein coat, it is still infective and can produce clones when introduced into a host bacterium.

GENE SPLICING

Enzymes

The task of selecting an individual gene and splicing it into a suitable vector was made easier by the discovery of a group of fascinating enzymes which act like biological glue and scissors. These extremely precise tools have become indispensable to the biochemist.

In 1967, researchers in several laboratories simultaneously discovered an enzyme they called DNA ligase. This enzyme helps in the joining of the two DNA chains that make up the double helix. Studies indicated that ligase repaired damaged DNA by closing "nicks" in the phosphate backbone of the DNA molecule. It acted almost like a proofreader verifying the accuracy of DNA replication. Here was the ideal glue for the splicing of DNA chains in genetic recombination.

Another group of enzymes, the restriction enzymes, proved to be the ideal scissors. Each kind of restriction enzyme recognizes a specific base sequence in double-helical DNA, and cleaves both strands of the molecule at a very specific site called the cleavage site, usually within this sequence. Restriction enzymes are found in a wide variety of bacteria where they protect the cell, destroying foreign DNA by cleaving it into small pieces. The cell's own DNA is not damaged because the site that would otherwise be recognized by its own restriction enzymes as a cleavage site is slightly altered by an additional group of atoms.

Of great importance is the fact that the base sequences at the cleavage site are palindromic. A palindrome is any word or phrase that reads the same backwards as forwards. The word "radar" and the phrase "Madam, I'm Adam" are both palindromes. The restriction enzyme called EcoR1, for example, cleaves the following sequence:

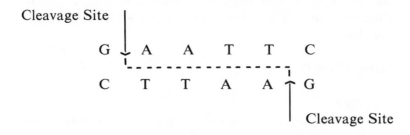

Cleavage Site

Cleavage Site

Here, as usual, the bases in the DNA molecule are represented by their first letter: A for adenine, T for thymine, C for cytosine, and G for guanine. The staggered cuts made by this enzyme sever the two sets of bases, each of which is a palindrome for the other. The severed DNA molecule opens up at the cleavage sites to form complementary single-strand sequences at its ends. (See Figure 2, page 32.)

Sticky Ends
The ends of a DNA molecule that has been cleaved by a restriction enzyme are called "sticky" because they will combine with, or stick to, a complementary sequence of bases on another single-stranded DNA molecule. The cohesive nature of the sticky ends has proved indispensable in creating new DNA molecules.

A vector in a DNA recombinant procedure can be prepared, for example, by using the EcoR1 restriction enzyme to cleave a plasmid at a unique site. The fragment of DNA to be inserted in the plasmid is also prepared by cleaving a large DNA molecule with the same EcoR1 restriction enzyme. The ends of this fragment would be complementary to those of the cut plasmid. When the fragment and the vector are mixed together, the sticky ends "anneal" the molecules together. The reaction usually takes place in the presence of DNA ligase, our molecular glue, which catalyzes the joining of the two ends.

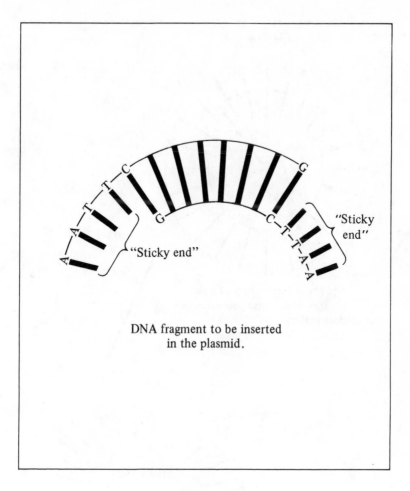

DNA fragment to be inserted
in the plasmid.

Figure 1

To help visualize the process, figures 1, 2, and 3 show the DNA fragment and the plasmid after having been cleaved at the specific sequence recognized by EcoR1.

In the presence of DNA ligase, the sticky ends will join to form a recombinant plasmid into which a foreign DNA fragment has been spliced (Figure 3).

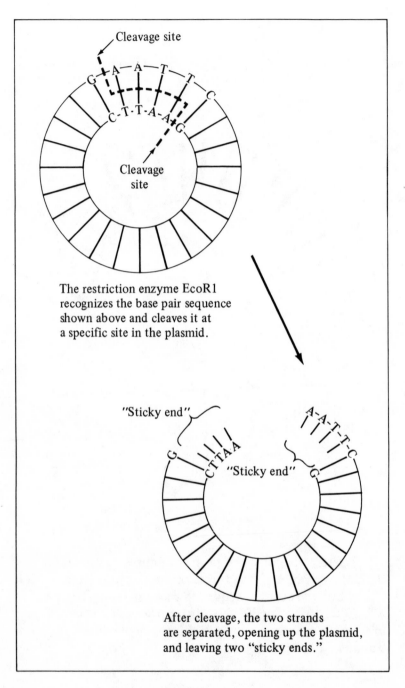

Cleavage site

Cleavage site

The restriction enzyme EcoR1
recognizes the base pair sequence
shown above and cleaves it at
a specific site in the plasmid.

"Sticky end"

"Sticky end"

After cleavage, the two strands
are separated, opening up the plasmid,
and leaving two "sticky ends."

Figure 2

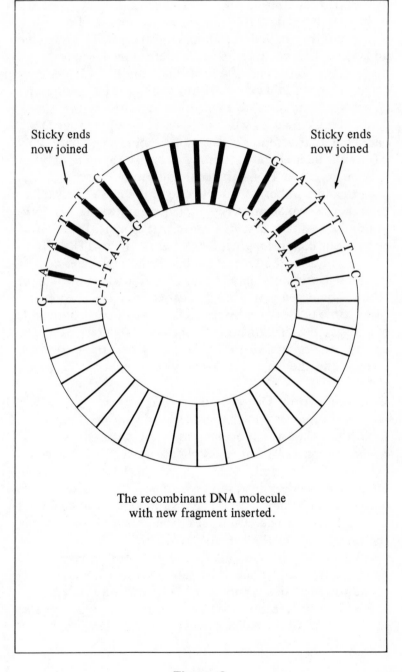

Sticky ends
now joined

Sticky ends
now joined

The recombinant DNA molecule
with new fragment inserted.

Figure 3

Terminal Transferase

A second method of splicing genes makes use of an interesting enzyme called terminal transferase. This enzyme adds a tail, consisting of a predetermined sequence of nucleotides, to the end of one of the strands of a DNA molecule. The tail is usually about a hundred units long and consists of one specific nucleotide repeated many times. Thus, a tail called poly dA consists of a fragment of DNA backbone that contains a string of adenine bases only. Poly dT would be a chain containing the base thymine only.

To join two DNA molecules, terminal transferase is used to add a tail of poly dA to one of them, and poly dT to the other. Since adenine is complementary to the base thymine, the two tails are, in a sense, sticky ends. In the presence of our biological glue, DNA ligase, the two DNA molecules will anneal and become one large molecule.

A variation of this method is to add short strands of DNA, about ten units long, consisting of base sequences susceptible to cleavage by restriction enzymes, to both ends of a large DNA fragment. When these so called linkers are cut by the appropriate restriction enzyme, sticky ends are formed and the fragment is ready to be spliced.

Genes of Higher Organisms

An interesting recent attempt to clone a rat insulin gene in *E. coli* has shown that even animal cell genes can be introduced into bacteria and can replicate there. Since the genes of higher organisms, unlike those of bacteria, contain introns (noncoding intervening sequences), a special technique had to be developed. The insulin gene itself could not be used, since a bacterium lacks the enzymes for cleaving the introns out of the primary RNA transcript.

Using an enzyme called reverse transcriptase which had been isolated from certain tumor viruses, a method was found to synthesize the insulin DNA from an mRNA template. The reverse transcriptase has the ability to reverse the usual DNA-to-RNA flow of information which had been the central dogma of molecular biology. Mature mRNA was taken from the pancreas of a rat so that the introns had already been removed. Insulin DNA was then synthesized from this messenger and was in a form which the bacteria could use. Several bacterial clones transformed with this so called cDNA (complementary DNA) were found to have synthesized small amounts of a simple form of insulin.

New Research Frontiers

New techniques, such as microinjecting a single gene's DNA directly into a mammalian cell nucleus, hold great promise for ultimately contributing to the cure of human genetic diseases.

Another technique that has proven useful for the production of small, simple proteins, is to synthesize the corresponding DNA molecule directly in the laboratory. The sequence of bases on the DNA can be predicted by knowing the structure of the protein and working backwards with the genetic code. A DNA molecule consisting of forty-two bases has been constructed, for example, to dictate the making of somatostatin, a small hormone consisting of fourteen amino acids.

An extremely controversial approach to recombinant technique is the so called shotgun method. Here, the entire genome of a cell is chopped up by restriction enzymes. The fragments are then indiscriminately mixed with vectors and, by transformation, introduced into bacteria. Thousands of bacterial cultures, forming a "library" of gene sequences of the organism, are then screened to find the desired product.

This technique, which led to the isolation of the human interferon gene, is considered potentially hazardous because scientists cannot tell what repressed or unknown functions of the DNA might cause unexpected problems. Until recently, shotgun methods were confined to P4 lab facilities, and even today they are severly restricted.

4
Patents, Products, and Projections

PATENTS ON LIVING ORGANISMS

In 1972, the United States Patent Office received a surprising request. General Electric Company wanted to patent a new form of life, an organism born in the company's laboratories. Its creator, Ananda M. Chakrabarty, took plasmids from three bacteria known for their ability to break up hydrocarbons and transferred them to a pseudomonas bacterium. The brand-new pseudomonas would have the power to clean up oil spills and would die off after having no more petroleum to devour.

Patent officials were at a loss. Could a live organism be patented? Crossbred plant or animal strains such as racehorses and hybrid tomatoes had never been protected by patenting. The officials concluded that their legal mandate did not extend to granting patents on living bacteria.

General Electric took its case to the courts. In June 1980, the Supreme Court voted five to four in favor of granting patents on life created in the laboratory. In the words of Justice Burger, the issue was "not between living and inanimate things, but between products of nature—whether living or not—and human-made inventions."

The first American patent on a living organism was granted in February, 1981, while G.E.'s patent was still pending. The award was made to Bristol Myers Company and three of its staff scientists. Streptosporangium, as their creation is called, produces carminomycin, an antibiotic antitumor agent. The patent for the pure cultured organism was added to an earlier patent for the process by which the drug is made.

MICROBES AND INDUSTRY

Actually, microorganisms have been beneficial to humans throughout history. Bacteria, yeasts, and molds have long helped us make familiar products such as cheese, bread, beer, wine, pickles, yogurt, and soy sauce. To these we must add a more recent discovery, antibiotics, now often derived from actinomycetes, yet another class of microscopic life.

Today, modern industrial microbiologists can vastly extend traditional fermentation techniques by recombinant DNA and other procedures. The ability to alter genetic information makes the uses of microorganisms seem almost limitless.

For thousands of years, the forces that converted milk to cheese or juice to alcohol remained secret and mysterious. Even after Anton van Leeuwenhoek, the seventeenth-century microscopist, saw tiny life forms under his lens, the actions of these "animalcules" were not understood. It took the work of several nineteenth-century scientists—Louis Pasteur foremost among them—to notice the role of microbes both in food manufacture and food spoilage.

Ultimately, it was found that colonies of microbes produce enzymes during their metabolic life processes. The enzymes promote chemical reactions in the surrounding medium. This is the effect we observe when milk turns sour or juice alcoholic.

Because different organisms release different enzymes, each fermentation product requires a perfectly pure culture. For example, Pasteur discovered that a certain brand of beer tasted sour because lactic-acid-producing bacteria had contaminated the yeast mixture in the brewing vats.

In World War I, chemical shortages gave rise to a new branch of industrial microbiology, one not concerned with food. Bacterial cultures in huge fermenting vessels converted carbohydrates into glycerol and acetone. These substances were needed for explosives and munitions.

The development of antibiotics came in the mid-twentieth century. Penicillin, the earliest of the "wonder drugs," is prepared from a mold. More recent products—the various "mycins"—are obtained from actinomycetes.

The Microbial Labor Force

The world is inhabited by thousands of microorganisms. Several hundred of these are our useful allies. Only a few are harmful to us. The rest hardly affect us at all.

The useful organisms can be divided into four classes: single cell bacteria, actinomycetes, molds, and yeasts. Single-cell bacteria and actinomycetes are prokaryotes. They have no nuclear membrane and only one chromosome. Molds and yeasts are eukaryotes. They have a nuclear membrane and more than one chromosome.

Micoorganisms make excellent workers. Their metabolism rate is high, which means that they quickly convert nutrients into various biological substances. They also reproduce very quickly. *E. coli*, for example, divide about three times an hour. Microorganisms are hardy. Some live without air, others near the freezing or boiling point of water, still others in salt water. Some will go dormant for years when circumstances are unfavorable, but become active as soon as conditions are right. Because they are so adaptable, they may be cultured in inexpensive media such as molasses or waste products of the corn and sugar industries.

Nowadays, microorganisms are grown not only for their conversion products (alcohol, for example) and for their metabolic products (such as the various enzymes they can synthesize); they are also grown as a food source in themselves. Processed into a tasteless flour called single-cell protein (SCP), they make an enriching additive to animal feed.

Stepping Up Production
Several techniques now multiply the uses and raise the industrial yield of microorganisms. First, accidental as well as induced mutations make it possible to select more productive bacterial strains. Protoplast fusion is another new approach. This is a way of crossing species by removing their cell walls, mixing the cell material, and allowing the wall to regenerate in the resultant organism.

Another technique is plasmid amplification—a way to force plasmids in a cell to multiply at a hundred times their normal rate. This enables scientists to implant a gene coding for a certain protein in a plasmid, then to amplify the plasmid, and thus to obtain a greatly increased output of the desired protein.

Finally, of course, the ability to transfer genetic characteristics from one organism to another enables scientists to create modified organisms with any number of desirable traits.

THE FUTURE
The use of microbes in industry has many advantages. Instead of requiring extreme temperatures for heating and cooling, as well as highly polluting solvents, microbes require only warmth, salts, and water. Unlike standard chemical conversions, biological conversions create few wasteful by-products because the organisms can be directed to target only one chemical reaction. The low cost of the culturing media on which microbes grow is also welcomed by manufacturers.

Products
Microbial methods may eventually replace traditional manufacturing techniques for many biological products. One substance already harvested in large quantities from

microorganisms is Xanthan gum, a long-chain molecule made up of repeated sugar units. Formerly, Xanthan was derived from plants, particularly from seaweed. Xanthan has various commercial uses. As a thickener and stabilizer it is not only added to many foods but also to drilling mud in oil well construction, to cosmetics, and to pharmaceuticals.

Bio-methods are likely to become important in making liquid and gaseous fuels. Wood, grain, corn, sugar cane—even municipal garbage and human wastes—can be converted to combustible fuel by bacteria specifically designed to break down each material.

Bacteria as "cleanup squads" for oil spills and chemical dumps already exist. Other, mineral-dissolving, strains are at work "mining" rare metals such as uranium and copper. (The metals are leached out of the soil by a kind of digestive action.) One long-range project is to use microbes as catalysts in converting natural substances such as glucose into raw material for textile fibers. Some companies are also planning to use genetically engineered microorganisms for such diverse purposes as making natural fructose (an intensified sweetener), propylene oxide (a chemical used to manufacture plastics), gasohol (a fuel composed of gasoline and alcohol), fertilizers, insecticides, and many other compounds.

Hormones

Biologic substances used in medicine and pharmacology are the first genetically engineered products to reach the market. A recently discovered substance, interferon, can now be produced through genetic engineering. This substance, which the body produces naturally in minute quantities, is believed to be effective against the viruses that cause hepatitis, rabies, herpes, and shingles. It may also play a role in fighting cancer. Interferon can be engineered in yeast cells as well as in bacteria. It is actually a general name for an entire family of substances. Some types of interferon may turn out to be more effective than others in treating specific diseases.

The first hormones to be produced by genetically manipulated bacteria are insulin and growth hormone. Insulin is normally secreted by the pancreas to regulate the amount of sugar in the body. More than a million Americans, though, suffer from insulin deficiency (diabetes) and require daily supplementary injections. Pharmaceutical insulin, until now derived from pig, beef cattle and sheep pancreas, occasionally causes undesirable side effects. The new product is less likely to do so.

As for growth hormone, the human pituitary gland produces it in very small quantities. To treat one child's growth deficiency for one year, the product of fifty human pituitary glands is needed. Now, experts hope to produce enough growth hormone in bacterial colonies to treat many more children and also to use it in healing fractures, burnt-tissue, cartilage injuries, and stomach ulcers.

Vaccines and Antibodies

Gene splicing is expected to produce many types of vaccines more cheaply and effectively than traditional methods. An even more revolutionary approach to understanding and treating disease may come through the use of monoclonal antibodies. These antibodies come from specialized clones of cells and parallel the body's own defenses against invasion by foreign elements. There are assumed to be hundreds of antibody types, each capable of striking one specific target. Monoclonal antibodies are so pure and specialized that they can even distinguish, for example, between six different forms of measles virus or between the red cells that compose different blood types. They can be used as probes and tracers to map parts of the body and to attack particular diseases.

The technique used to make monoclonal antibodies is cell fusion. An organism, usually a mouse, is injected with an antigen, a substance that stimulates the production of a specific antibody. The cells that produce the antibody are removed from the animal's spleen and fused with a fast growing cancerous kind of cell. The resultant fused cells or hybridomas are grown in tissue culture. They possess both the capacity for rapid growth and for producing the antibody originally stimulated by the antigen. Continuous "farming" of such a culture permits harvesting of specific antibodies as needed. Cloned antibodies may eventually replace vaccines to confer immunity to a host of infectious illnesses. Scientists also hope to use them as tumor detectors and as carriers for cancer-fighting chemicals.

New Work on Cancer

How does a normal cell become a cancer cell? The change may be triggered by a gene. Cancer cells behave quite differently from normal cells. For one thing, they escape the controls that prevent cells from invading adjoining tissues in the body. Perhaps some day gene manipulation will reverse the process and turn cancer cells back to normal again.

A few years ago, researchers found that some animal cancers were caused by viruses. They also found that the genes causing the cancer were originally normal animal genes. Somehow, these genes had been "stolen" from the animal by the virus. After being normally active in the process of cell differentiation, genes of this kind seem to "turn off" when their work is done. It is thought that some mechanism turns them on again when the virus carries them into new cells. As a result, the host cells become cancerous. Scientists refer to these genes as transforming genes.

Recently, though, scientists at several research laboratories have isolated transforming genes from several types of human cancer cells. At Cold Spring Harbor, researchers found a gene common to colon and lung tumors. At MIT, transforming genes were isolated from bladder and colon cancers as well as from human leukemia. These genes transform cultured normal mammalian cells into cancer cells.

Now that such a gene has been isolated, the next step is to observe its precise role in forming tumors. Probably, the transforming gene is only a link in a complex chain of reactions. But scientists are cautiously optimistic. One researcher hopes that people might eventually take a blood test to find out if they were carrying an active tumor gene. If so, treatment could begin before any tumors had actually started.

A New Green Revolution?

Biogenetic engineers are developing vaccines and hormones for animals as well as for humans. These and scores of other products and techniques promise to give an enormous boost to agriculture. Increased food production may parallel that of the mid-twentieth century, when newly developed antibiotics, hormones, pesticides, and fertilizers brought about the so called Green Revolution.

A vaccine against hoof-and-mouth disease is first in order of priority for international dairy, cattle, sheep, and hog farmers. The highly contagious disease produces sores in the mouths and hooves of animals, weakening them severely enough to make them agriculturally useless. It spreads rapidly and can be transmitted to humans. America has eliminated hoof-and-mouth disease by slaughtering all affected herds. But constant vigilance is needed to prevent the virus from being brought in again by travelers or foods from abroad.

Although traditional vaccines already exist, better ones are needed. Hoof-and-mouth disease is actually caused by some sixty related virus types and subtypes. The first hoof-and-mouth disease vaccine developed by recombinant techniques consists of a protein called VP3, one of the four proteins that make up the virus's surface. The protein is spliced into the genes of *E. coli* bacteria and cultured. The new vaccine is specific for only one of the many virus types, but the company that developed it is working on an inexpensive vaccine that will combat the entire range of viral strains at once.

On another front of dairy and livestock farming, animal growth hormones, manufactured by gene-spliced bacteria, may soon be used to increase milk and meat production. The growth-promoting drugs farmers have used for decades tend to remain in the meat that comes to our table. Possibly, the genetically engineered product will raise meat and milk yields and not leave residues harmful to human consumers.

Also on the horizon are disease- and pest-resistant plants grown from cloned cells or tissue cultures. Two giant food-processing companies are pursuing this path. One is trying to develop a better potato for its potato chip products, the other to make a better tomato for its canned soups. Genetic engineers in Germany even combined genes of both these vegetables and came up with a "pomato" plant that grows potatoes at the roots and tomatoes on its branches.

The engineering of plants is complicated because plants may have as many as ten thousand genes—far more than the bacteria used in other recombinant designs. All the same, the groundwork has been laid. American researchers recently managed to transfer a gene from a French bean seed into a sunflower cell, where it is expected to produce a certain protein. The gene was spliced into a bacterium that usually infects plants with gall disease. Its infectious mechanism makes it useful as a vehicle. The scientists called their product sunbean. Entire sunbean plants regenerated from this single recombinant cell could serve as an extra-high-protein food.

Most dramatic of all is the development of self-fertilizing plant strains, which experts envision in the not-too-distant future. Contemporary agriculture uses enormous quantities of nitrogen-based fertilizers to increase crop yields. Not only are these fertilizers costly but they tend to pollute streams and ground water. Nitrogen, an essential substance for all growing plants, is a gas freely available in the atmosphere. Plants can only absorb it, though, when it has been changed to ammonia by so called nitrogen-fixing bacteria in the soil.

Scientists at Cornell University have isolated the group of genes in bacteria that enable them to fix nitrogen and have spliced these into yeast cells. The genes remain stable during many divisions of their host cells and resume nitrogen-fixing activity when they are spliced back again into their native bacteria. Until now, experimenters have not induced yeast to fix nitrogen. Research is pushing ahead, though, toward the day when recombinant techniques will produce nitrogen-fixing strains of wheat, corn, and other food plants.

Mail-Order Genes

If you wish to buy a test tube full of viral DNA, some infected tissue-culture cells, or a few cubic centimeters of restriction enzymes, you can order all these and more from a gene splicing supply company.

Mail-ordered biological parts have facilitated genetic engineering, and so have automated processing machines. Gene recombination by hand is difficult and slow. In the past, the time and expense involved created research bottlenecks. Early in 1981, though, new apparatus developed by several firms made gene splicing and assembly quick and easy. Controlled by microprocessors, polynucleotide assembly machines make chains of genetic fragments to exact specifications. The short strands thus assembled are used as probes for finding the corresponding genes in large collections of genetic material.

"Gene machines" add one nucleotide after another onto a rigid column of support material in the order dictated by a programming card. Because they can add a subunit every thirty minutes or so, the machines finish in a few hours what used to take months to accomplish.

Instruments of this kind can find, snip, and reassemble genes, change their hereditary messages, and redesign them to order, all under the supervision of an operator who needs relatively little training.

Speeding up gene assembly also speeds up the job of mapping the human genome. Several organizations now compile decoded gene messages from research labs all over the world. One of the largest of these gene libraries has been assembled by the National Biomedical Research Foundation. By late 1980, the specific location of approximately 342 genes had already been pinpointed on human chromosomes. Thousands more remain to be mapped, however.

The Frozen Zoo

Today's endangered animal and plant species may yet be saved from total extinction by deep-frozen cells and seeds deposited in gene banks. At the San Diego, California, zoo, cells of hundreds of animals lie stored in plastic vials immersed in liquid nitrogen. It is hoped that some time in the future, experts will be able to coax them back to life and induce them to grow and multiply. In danger of extinction before the end of the century are the giant panda, the rhinoceros, the Siberian tiger, and scores of other creatures driven out by humans.

Gene banking can prevent inbreeding of captive animals by preserving specimens from a wider gene pool. Eventually, techniques may be perfected whereby frozen sperm and ova can be thawed, combined in a test tube to form an embryo, and implanted in the surrogate womb of another animal until birth.

CLONING—IN FACT AND FICTION

Making a human clone would be such a sensational feat that one might think every molecular biologist must be trying to accomplish it. In reality, this is not so at all. Cloning—the asexual reproduction of an organism in which the offspring is the result of a single parental cell—is primarily an important research tool.

Asexual reproduction is not uncommon in nature. It is found in plants that grow from cuttings, in single-celled organisms that reproduce by dividing, and in certain jellyfish that reproduce by budding. The phenomenon in which offspring develop from the nucleus of an unfertilized egg is called parthenogenesis, from the Greek *parthenos*, meaning "virgin," and *genesis*, meaning "origin." Male bees, for example, are formed this way. They are the sons of the queen bee alone. Parthenogenesis sometimes occurs in birds and, occasionally, in mammals such as hamsters and mice. This kind of accidental mammalian parthenogenesis, though, results in only a few rudimentary cells and never goes far enough to produce a complete animal.

Several dozen plants can now be propagated by cloning. That is, they are regenerated from single cells in tissue culture. Among them are strawberries, asparagus, and pineapple, as well as African violets and carnations. The carnivorous plant Venus's-flytrap, almost entirely driven out of its natural habitat, is about to be saved for posterity by being cloned.

To clone plants, growers place minute slivers of a parent plant in nutrient broth for several months. Eventually, the cells multiply, and when these cells are transplanted they put down roots. Commercial growers find this cultivating method practical. A stock of tissue culture 2 feet (0.6 m) square can turn out twenty thousand plants. Another advantage of this method is the rapid rate at which seedlings grow. This is due to the hormones surrounding the tissues as they lie in the culture bath. In the future, this method may be widely applied in forestry as well as in agriculture.

Three Cloned Mice

Cloning a mammal differs from parthenogenesis. It does not begin with the nucleus of an egg cell, but with the nucleus of a single body cell. An egg cell is used, but only as a carrier or incubator for a foreign cell nucleus.

In 1981, the first successful mouse cloning experiments were reported from Switzerland and the United States. Cell nuclei were taken from the inner cell-mass of a gray mouse embryo at an early stage of fetal development. Each nucleus was inserted into the freshly fertilized egg of a black mouse. The original nuclear material was immediately removed from the eggs to leave only the new material. After culturing the eggs for a few days, researchers transferred them to the wombs of white mice made ready for pregnancy by treatment with hormones.

In one experimental setup 542 transplants were performed. From these, only three mice resulted which could be recognized as true clones. Two were female, one male. They were, of course, gray like their parent. Studies of cultured tissue samples and enzyme analysis showed that they were in all respects like the donor of the nuclei and not like the donor of the egg or the surrogate mother who carried them in her womb.

Cloning the cell nuclei of a young embryo works because these cells have hardly yet begun to differentiate. Efforts to clone cells from an animal at a later stage of development have not yet succeeded. Perhaps cell differentiation during fetal development is an irreversible process. Until the experiment of the three cloned mice, successful cloning had been performed only with frogs and other amphibians who have the ability to regenerate lost body parts under certain conditions. The fact that mice, too, are clonable suggests that perhaps mammals, humans among them, might have kept vestiges of this valuable trait.

Human Cloning

The complicated steps and low success rate in cloning a mouse make one realize what it would take to clone a man or woman. A book published in 1978, David Rorvik's *In His Image—The Cloning of a Man*, claimed to be a factual report on the genetic copying of a baby boy, an exact duplicate of his millionaire father. In fact, it describes all the steps of mouse cloning, from nuclear transfer to gestation in a surrogate womb, except that the cell donor is a human adult. Though it makes interesting reading, the book comes closer to science fiction than to actuality. Of all the obstacles in the way of this enormous undertaking, cell differentiation in the adult body is the most formidable.

As yet, the farthest science has gone toward cloning a person is to clone parts of a human X chromosome. The cloned fragment constitutes about one percent of the entire chromosome. The other ninety-nine percent have yet to be assembled. Normal humans have twenty-three chromosome pairs. In females, the twenty-third pair consists of two X chromosomes; in males the corresponding pair holds one X and one Y. In the experiment, fragments of X chromosome were spliced and grown in bacteria. The method enables scientists to reproduce large quantities of such fragments for study.

Investigators are eager to learn, for example, why and how one of the two X chromosomes in females normally turns off after fetal development and becomes inactive. The answer should throw light on the secrets of cell regulation in general.

5
Human Genetic Therapy

Can human genes be engineered like those of microorganisms? Some people fear this possibility, while others hope for it. Those who fear it disapprove of interference with the basic processes of heredity. They consider such experiments hazardous and believe that matters until now in the hands of natural selection should not be controlled by humans. Those who welcome the possibility look forward to a better understanding of hereditary disorders as well as to their prevention and possible cure.

We live in an age when many killing and crippling childhood diseases have been brought under control by vaccines. Unfortunately, however, some five thousand different genetic defects still take a heavy toll. Each year, their impact brings sadness and hardship to many families.

Until recently, there was no help for the accidents of biological inheritance. People had no influence over the great genetic lottery. Now, however, genetic medicine is developing new options for prospective parents. Many birth defects can be prevented. Some may be diagnosed in the unborn fetus. Others may even be treated successfully—before or after birth.

Although human genetic surgery is still experimental, current practices such as genetic testing, counseling, and therapy promise to relieve some of humanity's most dreaded disabilities.

A CASE HISTORY

Several years ago, Susan and David M. discovered that they were about to become parents in their late thirties, at a time of life when many couples were already seeing their children through high school. Unfortunately, the child that was born was not normal: the baby girl's face and internal organs were malformed. Her eyes were fused together, her nose flattened, her palate cleft. She had difficulty breathing, her kidneys were misplaced, and she was unable to urinate. One week later, the baby died. During her short life, teams of doctors attempted to rescue her by various surgical techniques. Had she lived, she would have been mentally retarded and physically disabled.

Today, a couple like Mr. and Mrs. M. is less likely to suffer the same catastrophe. The attending physician would point out that a woman who is close to forty runs nearly a three percent risk of giving birth to a child with chromosomal abnormalities. The doctor would undoubtedly tell the expectant mother about a process called amniocentesis which allows experts to examine the amniotic fluid surrounding the fetus in the womb. Analysis of this fluid will reveal many genetic disorders if they are present. Usually, the test is conducted between the fourteenth and twentieth weeks of pregnancy.

If Susan had undergone amniocentesis, a chromosome count would have revealed that the cells of the expected baby carried forty-seven instead of forty-six chromosomes. Specifically, there were three number thirteen chromosomes instead of the usual pair. Although such abnormalities are not yet remediable, prenatal testing would have offered the parents a chance to decide whether or not to carry the pregnancy to term.

THE MECHANISM OF HEREDITY

To understand the many causes of birth defects it is helpful to review the mechanism of human heredity. As you already know, the genes of plants and animals are ranged along fibrous structures called chromosomes. They are composed mainly of DNA and protein and located in the nucleus of every dividing cell except red blood cells.

Each kind of plant and animal has its own specific number of chromosomes in all its cells. Humans have forty-six chromosomes or, rather, twenty-three pairs. Of each pair, one chromosome has been inherited from the mother and one from the father.

Human Gene Structure

While chromosomes can be seen under a powerful micro-scope, the genes which command the cells' behavior are far too small to be visible. Their existence can only be inferred by their activities and by certain chemical probes. Cytologists (specialists in the study of cells) are still uncertain how many genes are located within our 23 pairs of chromosomes. Estimates range from 500,000 to over a million. Even though all our cells, with rare exceptions, contain the same number of chromosomes, the cells are widely different in function. Some cells make up the brain, others the intestine, still others function as skin or as blood. Just how this differentiation begins during the embryo's development and just how it is maintained, remains a mystery to scientists.

Sexual Reproduction

To start a new human life, twenty-three chromosomes from a man must join twenty-three chromosomes from a woman. How is this accomplished when each individual's cells contain twice that number? The reproductive cells, also called germ cells, produced by the testes in men and the ovaries in women, undergo meiosis, or reduction division. In meiosis the cell divides twice, but the chromosomes duplicate only once. As a result, the male and female germ cells are haploid, which means that they contain half the usual number of chromosomes.

The genetic makeup of men and women differs in only one chromosome. Twenty-two pairs, the so called autosomes, are identical in the cells of both sexes. The twenty-third pair, the sex chromosomes, consist of two X chromosomes in females (XX) and of an X and a Y in males (XY). Genetic disorders in any of the twenty-two autosomes are called autosomal disorders. Those residing in the sex chromosomes are called X-linked. No Y-linked disorders have been discovered.

The Y chromosome is small and seems to contain little genetic information besides that for determining male gender. The X chromosomes, being large, carry more information and more chance of abnormality.

Any accident, however slight, in germ cell division of one parent may result in a severe birth defect. If division is not completely equal, if even a single extra chromosome either leaves the cell or remains inside, the effect may be devastating after the cell becomes joined to its partner of the opposite sex and begins developing into an embryo.

Chromosome Errors

Errors in chromosome number are thought to account for forty percent of miscarriages in the first three months of pregnancy. In some cases, though, the error is less severe and the fetus survives in spite of a serious handicap. A commonly known condition resulting from an extra chromosome in the twenty-first pair is Down's syndrome. Children born with this affliction are mentally retarded, small in stature, and lacking normal fingerprints. Typically, their eyes are somewhat slanted, which is the reason this condition was formerly named mongoloidism.

Another disorder, known as fragile X, has been recently diagnosed. This condition, which is thought to be about half as common as Down's syndrome, is associated with extreme fragility of the X chromosome. It results in mental retardation and affects male children only. Females are not affected, for they have a second X chromosome to fall back on.

Traditionally, geneticists have held that the greatest risk of chromosome abnormality is to be expected in women past the age of thirty-five. A woman's egg cells are formed before she is born. This means that in a woman of forty the eggs are a little over forty years old. A man's sperm cells, on the other hand, are formed continually.

New studies show, however, that the largest number of children with Down's syndrome are actually born to young mothers. It has also been discovered that the extra chromosome 21 is often supplied by the father. Further, advanced age in fathers appears to be responsible for many genetic mutations of yet another kind. In future, when testing has become simplified and perfected, genetic screening for expectant parents of all ages and both sexes may become routine.

DOMINANT AND RECESSIVE TRAITS

Back in the nineteenth century, when Mendel worked on his pea-plant experiments, he started out by breeding pairs of pure plant lines each chosen for a particular characteristic. For example, he bred tall plants and dwarf plants, plants that produced only green seed pods and plants that produced only yellow seed pods, plants whose seeds were smooth and plants whose seeds were wrinkled. Fortunately peas grow fast, because he had to watch and wait for many generations of pea plants to make sure they bred true to their parental type.

When Mendel was certain his plants were breeding perfectly true, he went on to cross-pollinate some of them, keeping careful records of the results. For instance, he would remove the stamens (the male part) of a tall plant so that it could not fertilize itself. Then he brushed its pistils (the female part) with pollen from a dwarf plant. He called the resulting offspring a hybrid.

Contrary to popular expectation, hybrids did not show a blending of their parents' traits. A tall plant crossed with a short one did not produce a medium-sized hybrid. Instead, one characteristic asserted itself, while the other seemed to disappear. Hybrids of tall and dwarf plants were all tall; hybrids of yellow-seeded and green-seeded plants all bore yellow seeds; and so it was with the other plants in the experiment. As Mendel termed it, one trait was dominant, the other recessive.

What happened in the next generation of pea plants was even more surprising. The plants grown from yellow hybrid seeds did not breed true, that is, they were not all the same color as their parental stock. Approximately one of every four seeds produced by these new plants was not yellow but green.

Mendel kept careful records, labeled his seeds, and went on planting. Observing the next few generations, he noted that green seeds (recessive) grew only green-seeded plants. Of the yellow seeds (dominant), about one third bred true for yellow-seeded plants. The other yellow seeds again produced yellow and green seeds in a three to one ratio.

These observations led to Mendel's discovery that each plant inherits *two* factors for a trait such as seed color: one from the male and one from the female parent. If each parent carries both dominant and recessive characteristics, then four possible combinations can be passed down to the next generation. Take a look at the diagram drawn in terms of yellow (Y) and green (g) seeds. (We use a capital Y because yellow is dominant, and a small g for the recessive green.) Here, we are assuming that both parent plants are like Mendel's first-generation hybrids, each carrying one Y and one g factor.

Plants whose makeup is YY have yellow seeds, of course. But, because yellow is dominant, plants whose makeup is Yg or gY will also have yellow seeds. Two g-factors meeting, though, will have only green seeds (gg) and will always breed true.

You can see that there are three chances out of four (seventy-five percent) that the dominant factor will be expressed in the offspring, but only one chance out of four (twenty-five percent) that the recessive factor will be expressed.

From the diagram you can also tell that even though all the Y-carrying plants look alike, they may hold different inheritance factors. Scientists use the terms phenotype (to describe the appearance) and genotype (to describe the total genetic makeup) of organisms.

Today, Mendel's insights are still valid, although we know that inheritance works by a combination of many complex factors. Skin color in humans, for example, is determined by several genes, not by just one. Besides, skin is made up of five different layers. Therefore, unlike Mendel's pea seeds, each child of mixed parentage in terms of skin color, will have a uniquely shaded complexion, even though dark pigment is dominant.

We also know, now, that from time to time, in the replication process of cells, a small random change called mutation occurs. Mutations in germ cells (sex cells) are subject to the same laws as other inheritable traits. They may be dominant or recessive and can be passed on to future offspring.

Genetic Disorders

About 2,500 genetic diseases are caused by abnormality in a single gene. It might be located in one of the forty-four non-sex chromosomes (autosomal diseases) or in the X chromosome (X-linked). Over 2,000 more hereditary disorders are caused by defects in several genes (polygenic diseases). Abnormal births may also result from environmental factors such as toxic chemicals that enter through the mother's bloodstream, or from viral infections such as German measles contracted by the mother in early pregnancy. The latter disorders are congenital (present from birth) but not necessarily genetic (involving the genes).

Like other inheritable traits, genetic disorders may be dominant or recessive. A person who has inherited a recessive disorder from one parent is a carrier who may be completely free of symptoms. This is true, for instance, of people who carry one gene for albinism, a defect in the body's ability to form pigment in hair, skin, and eyes. If two carriers of this gene produce a child, however, chances are one in four, or twenty-five percent, that both will pass on their one defective gene. If this coincidence occurs, the child will be born with the whitish hair, colorless eyes, and poor vision of the albino.

Carriers of one gene for any particular condition are described as heterozygous (carrying mixed genes); carriers of both genes for a particular condition are called homozygous (carrying uniform genes).

Among the common autosomal dominant diseases are certain kinds of dwarfism, Huntington's chorea, polycystic kidneys, and the blindness-causing retinoblastoma. Autosomal recessive disorders include phenylketonuria (PKU), Tay-Sachs disease, and sickle-cell anemia. The latter three tend to run in certain population groups. They will be discussed in the section on preventive screening.

X-linked disorders are more threatening to males than to females. In a man, a single recessive gene mutation on the X chromosome produces disease because he has no second X to provide a normal compensating gene. A mother who is a carrier runs a fifty percent risk of passing down her defective gene. Since all her daughters receive the father's normal X chromosome, those who receive the mother's defective X will be carriers and those who receive the mother's normal X will be entirely normal. Those sons, however, who inherit their mother's abnormal X will have the disease.

If one of these sons should then become a father in spite of his illness, all his daughters will be carriers, since they all inherit his single abnormal X, while his sons will receive his Y and will therefore be unaffected. Some of the common X-linked recessive disorders are hemophilia, color blindness, and certain types of muscular dystrophy.

PRENATAL TESTING
In 1980, a team of surgeons at New York's Mount Sinai Hospital performed a bold and precarious maneuver on a patient pregnant with twins. Prenatal tests had shown that

one twin was in good health, while the other carried an extra chromosome 21. Pictures of the chromosomes of each fetus showed that both were male, that they were not genetically identical but were fraternal twins, that one seemed to be free of abnormalities while the other was afflicted with Down's syndrome. Not only would he be born retarded, but he was likely to be physically disabled. Four months before the twins were due to be born, surgeons destroyed the abnormal fetus without harming the normal twin.

Amniocentesis

The prologue to this procedure began a few months earlier with the process called amniocentesis, which enabled doctors to examine the chromosomes of the fetuses. The expectant mother was over forty and had previously not been able to conceive. This placed her in a high-risk category for fetal abnormalities. As in all such cases today, her obstetrician advised prenatal testing.

Amniocentesis is performed in a hospital operating room. To prevent injury to the fetus, doctors follow its exact position from moment to moment with a pulsed ultrasound scanning device. The surgeon inserts a thin, hollow needle through an anesthetized area in the mother's abdominal wall and into the amniotic sac, then draws out about 20 cubic centimeters (1.2 cu in) of amniotic fluid. This clear yellow liquid is the habitat in which the embryo floats until birth. It contains the embryo's urine as well as other body chemicals and cell materials. The procedure takes only a few minutes. The fluid is taken to the genetic laboratory where a karyotype is made.

Karyotyping

If, for any reason, you wanted to see a picture of your own chromosomes, you would find it surprisingly easy to obtain. Such a picture allows experts to count and examine the chromosomes to see if any are duplicated, missing, broken or misshapen. The picture, an enlarged and organized photograph of the chromosomes of a cell, is called a karyotype.

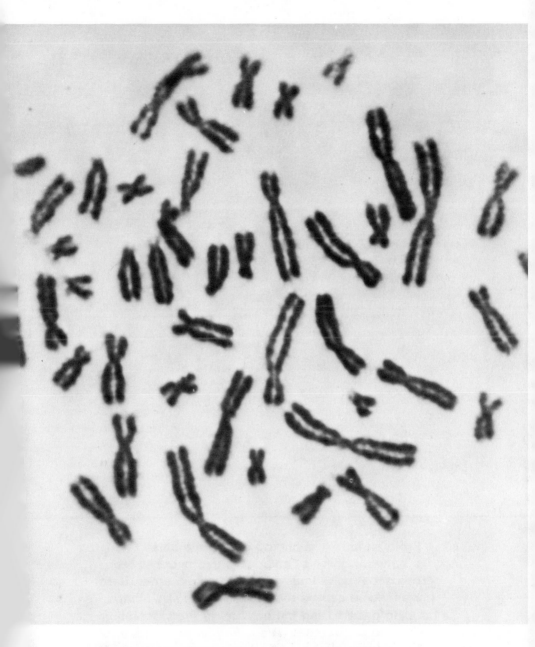

Chromosomes on a glass slide emerging from
a burst human cell. This enlarged photograph
is the first step in preparing a karyotype.

A NORMAL HUMAN KARYOTYPE

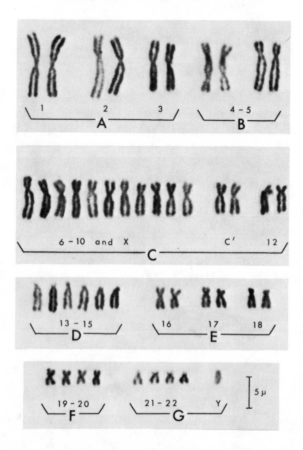

From an enlarged photograph of the burst cell,
a lab technician has snipped these twenty-three
chromosome pairs and arranged them in order. Each
chromosome can be recognized by its size, shape,
banding pattern, and the position of the indentation
called the centromere. The sex-determining factors
(XX or XY) are always placed last. Here, the X and Y
chromosomes show that the subject is male.

Usually, the sample to be examined comes from the patient's white blood cells or from a small patch of skin tissue.

When the patient is an unborn child, however, the cells for examination are cultured from amniotic fluid. A technician rushes the fluid from the operating room to the genetic laboratory in a small, flat-sided bottle. In the lab, a cytologist (cell specialist) places the bottle in an incubator at 37 degrees centigrade (98.6°F), which is body temperature. The bottle lies on its side. After a while, the fetal cells sink down and attach themselves to the bottom surface. A nutrient solution is added to help the cells multiply quickly. This part of the process is called "planting." Twice a week, the cytologist feeds the cells by cautiously removing the old solution under a sterile laboratory hood and adding fresh nutrients.

After two weeks, when enough cell colonies have formed, the process called "harvesting" begins. A chemical added to the bottle loosens the cells from the glass, and the mixture is centrifuged (spun at high speed) to remove all liquid, leaving only the pure cell culture.

Live cells are in constant internal change as they prepare for mitosis, the process by which they divide and multiply. At that moment which is best for observation, the cytologist adds a drop of mitotic inhibitor to stop further mitosis. A hypertonic solution comes next, to puff up and separate the cells so they are not closely packed. Now a special agent is dropped on the slide, which causes the cells to burst open and spew out their chromosomes. Then the chromosomes are treated with a fixative and stained.

Looking through a powerful microscope, a lab technician counts the chromosomes of about twenty of the cells in the sample. Then three burst cells that are perfectly clear are chosen to be photographed by an enlarging camera built into the microscope. Finally, the pictures of individual chromosomes from a single cell are snipped from the photograph and pasted in four rows of numbered pairs onto another sheet of paper. This is the karyotype.

Testing by Recombinant Techniques

A recombinant technique perfected in 1978 enables scientists to diagnose sickle cells and other genetic blood disorders in the unborn. The test uses as little as 15 milliliters (0.02 qt) of amniotic fluid. Without any further culturing, the fetal cells in the fluid are subjected to genetic analysis. A restriction enzyme picks out the specific site on the DNA strands where the hemoglobin gene is encoded, snipping out fragments that vary in size according to whether the gene is normal or abnormal. The test can also be applied to another hemoglobin disorder, alpha-thalassemia, which affects Mediterranean peoples.

Doctors hope that eventually this diagnostic technique will be applicable to an even wider range of inborn defects, including beta-thalassemia and muscular dystrophy. The problem is to find a specific probe for each particular trouble-causing gene.

Genetic Counseling

The doctor who takes care of a pregnant woman until after her baby is delivered may want to know many things about her and her husband: their age, their health, the health of previous children, of brothers and sisters and prospective grandparents. He may want to know their occupation and even the family's geographic and ethnic background. If answers to any of these questions raise concern about the well-being of the expected baby, the doctor may refer the couple to a genetic counseling service.

The genetic counselor constructs a "pedigree" of both sides of the family, taking into account all health abnormalities, lengths of life and causes of death. Medical examination of both parents is part of the complete routine, including X rays, biochemical analyses and analysis of the chromosomes by karyotype. If the outcome shows that this family is at high risk for some kind of abnormality in its descendants, the counselor may suggest amniocentesis, so that the fetus's amniotic fluid can be examined.

Karyotyping is not the only test performed on amniotic fluid. Another test investigates the cell-free fluid itself for the presence and amount of alpha-fetoprotein, a substance produced by the fetus until shortly after birth. Too much of this protein often indicates a malformation of the baby's brain and spinal cord. This can result in two very serious defects: "open spine" (spina bifida) and anencephaly. Anencephaly denotes the partial absence of brain and cranium, the "headless baby" syndrome which is always fatal. Victims of open spine often do survive but remain handicapped by weak or paralyzed legs, curved posture, and lack of bladder and bowel control.

Amniocentesis also enables doctors to detect some seventy-five metabolic disorders. Tests for these disorders are based on the fact that in the cells of an affected fetus various kinds of metabolic activities are likely to be abnormal, deficient, or altogether absent.

If a defect is indeed found, the genetic counselor will tell the parents what their options are, depending on the severity of the condition. In a few cases prenatal therapy is now possible and can be started immediately. In other cases, the child's disorder can be remedied with drugs or surgery. In a few cases where the condition leads to suffering and early death, parents may decide on an abortion.

Preventive Surgery
In the case just cited of the twin fetuses, one of which was abnormal, genetic counselors informed the parents of the hospital's findings. The mother feared that a retarded twin would impair the normal child's entire life. Backed up by the mother's determination and by a New York City Supreme Court opinion supporting her right to abort the abnormal fetus, surgeons at the hospital went ahead with the extremely delicate procedure.

Once again monitoring the positions of the two fetuses, the doctors punctured the heart of the abnormal one with a hollow needle, withdrew some blood, and stopped the heart from beating. A few months later, the normal baby was delivered in good health. A thin membrane of nonliving tissue was all that was left of the defective fetus.

Needless to say, the proceedings were highly controversial. Several members of the medical community publicly deplored the operation on moral and medical grounds. Others approved of the decision. They foresaw a hopelessly dependent life for the retarded child and sympathized with the prospective parents, who feared that the emotional and financial burden of the disabled brother's presence would affect the development of the healthy twin and the well-being of the entire family. Still others did not agree with the mother's decision, but felt, with the court, that she had the right to make this choice.

Preventive Screening

How can birth defects be prevented? Some enthusiasts of eugenics, the practice of human stock improvement, suggest storing a karyotype and genetic profile for every citizen in a central data bank. Every couple wishing to have children would consult the data and receive advice on the kind and degree of risk involved for their offspring. Perhaps they would be advised to adopt children rather than to produce their own. If they went ahead to give birth after all, they might be fined or taxed.

Few people want "Big Brother" to watch them quite so closely, however. Instead, mass screening of certain high-risk populations has recently been carried out in selected areas, as a public service.

SOME HEREDITARY
METABOLIC DISORDERS

Three inborn errors of metabolism due to single-gene defects have received wide attention. Each disorder occurs in certain particular populations more than in others. Each has been the subject of mass screening programs for the purpose of prevention, therapy, and further research.

Phenylketonuria (PKU)

In 1934, a Norwegian mother of two retarded children brought them to see a physician because she noticed that they carried a peculiar chemical odor. Chemical tests on their diapers showed that the children's urine turned blue in reaction to ferric chloride. The substance responsible proved to be phenylpyruvic acid, an abnormal metabolic product in the family of phenyl-ketones. In writing about the disease which he was the first to identify, the doctor named it phenylketonuria or PKU.

In the United States, only about one out of ten thousand infants is born with PKU; but about one person in fifty is a heterozygous carrier of the defect.

PKU is most often found in people of northern European origin. PKU patients tend to be pale complexioned, light blond and blue-eyed. Because of their inborn biochemical deficiency, they lack the enzyme to convert the amino acid phenylalanine into other needed compounds. Accumulations of phenylalanine in the brain prevent nourishment and development of brain cells. Therefore, if babies are not treated from early infancy, they succumb to increasing mental retardation, seizures, and skin lesions.

Since 1961, a rather simple test and a special diet have made PKU retardation preventable. Once detected, the disease is treated with a diet using specially treated milk protein in place of meat, milk, or cheese. Once rapid brain development is past, at about the age of six, the diet may safely be discontinued.

Formerly, PKU victims had been far too disabled to become parents. Now, with early treatment, they began leading normal lives. It appeared however, that PKU mothers tended to have severely retarded babies with tiny heads. Apparently, high concentrations of phenylalanine in the mother's body, though no longer harmful to her, caused havoc with the brain development of the fetus. We know, now, that to give birth to a healthy child, women who have PKU must resume their special diet months before they become pregnant.

Tay-Sachs Disease
More dreadful than PKU, because it is always fatal, is Tay-Sachs disease (TSD), an inherited enzyme deficiency tend-

ing to strike Jews of eastern European extraction. It affects about one in three thousand infants born to this population group. The disease is named after the two physicians who first analyzed and described it.

Victims of TSD are born in apparently perfect health. A few months later, though, they become weak, listless, and spastic. Their condition deteriorates during three or four years, until the end. Since there is still no cure for affected infants, screening for TSD must begin with future parents. Research has shown that one in twenty-five Jews of eastern European extraction carries this specific gene defect. Each time two carriers become parents, there is a twenty-five percent chance that their child will receive the defective gene from both father and mother, and thus become a victim of TSD.

When two known carriers of TSD decide to have a child, the mother usually undergoes amniocentesis early in pregnancy. If tests on the amniotic fluid show that the baby has TSD, abortion is the only preventive measure now available.

Sickle Cell Anemia

A third single-gene deficiency often subject to prenatal screening is sickle cell anemia (SCA). It is frequently found in people of African ancestry. SCA is caused by a genetic change in the protein hemoglobin, the body's oxygen-carrying molecule in red blood cells. Under certain low oxygen conditions, the blood cells cave in at the center and assume a sickle shape instead of their normal doughnut form. Severe anemia is one result. Another result can be blockage of small blood vessels and blood clots in vital organs.

Sickle cell patients suffer from painful and disabling attacks. These eventually lead to complications and death in early middle age. Mass screening has revealed that approximately one in twelve black Americans carries one gene for the disease and is therefore virtually unaffected. About one in six hundred, though, carries both genes and suffers from sickle cell symptoms.

There is some evidence that the disorder, which can also be found in Mediterranean people who inhabit swampy regions, is actually a defense mechanism conferring immunity to the worst effects of malaria.

Until recently, tests for sickle cells had to be performed on prospective parents rather than on the unborn child, because drawing blood from a fetus is difficult and risky. This meant that doctors could only estimate the degree to which the expected child might be affected. Now, however, recombinant techniques allow scientists to diagnose sickle cells by examining the amniotic fluid of the fetus.

HELP FOR THE UNBORN

Even when a certain defect has previously occurred in the family, expectant mothers and fathers sometimes prefer to hope for the best and await the outcome rather than to subject themselves and the child in the womb to extensive medical procedures. In great part, this is because the number of options for expectant parents of a defective child is still depressingly low. In many cases, abortion is the only alternative.

Fortunately, this unhappy state of things is changing. More and more, doctors are working on treatments for the unborn in the womb. For instance, certain life-threatening vitamin deficiencies caused by genetic defects can be treated by giving the mother large doses of the needed substance during her pregnancy. Another technique, used with infants expected to be premature, helps forestall respiratory disease and possible death: cortisone administered through the mother's bloodstream hastens maturing of the baby's lungs. Yet another technique is to administer digitalis to strengthen an unborn baby's heartbeat.

Genetic Surgery

The major breakthrough, though, which patients and parents all over the world look forward to, is genetic surgery. Indeed, there is a good chance that disabilities such as those caused by the lack of an enzyme will become curable by genetic engineering. This might be done by placing normal liver cells capable of making the enzyme into the fetal bloodstream. If all went according to plans, these cells would lodge in the fetal liver, multiply there, and take over production of the missing substance.

In a first step towards such a procedure, a group of scientists managed to microinject single genes into single mammalian cells and were pleased to observe that in at least one case the gene caused the cell to function normally.

The next step will be to correct defective cells in live mammals instead of *in vitro*. One laboratory has developed a valuable strain of mice carrying the genetic blood defect alpha-thalassemia. The mice will be used to study this disorder so that ways can be found to remedy it in humans.

Test Tube Parenthood
One out of five American couples of childbearing age is infertile. In sixty percent of cases the problem has been found to lie with the woman, in forty percent of cases, with the man. What can be done for people who are unable to have children in the usual way? A new reproductive technology is ready to come to their aid.

Strictly speaking, such procedures as banking of frozen sperm, artificial insemination, test tube fertilization, and embryo implantation in a surrogate mother's womb, cannot be classified under genetic engineering. The cell manipulations involve only the germ cells—sperm and egg—and leave the nuclei with their myriads of hereditary messages untouched. Yet reproductive engineering has obvious features in common with genetic engineering. Both seem to be in the business of manufacturing life, giving humans power over processes that have traditionally been subject to providence or fate.

Engineered reproduction is established practice in the livestock industry where breed improvement is of ultimate importance. In humans, the wish for children by the childless is often so desperate that the delicacy of the procedures and the emotional and ethical issues raised have not prevented steady expansion of the field.

Fifteen hundred American women become pregnant each year through artificial insemination by donor (AID). Sperm which has been frozen and stored is available from sperm banks. There are even organizations that sell sperm donated by members of specific groups, such as Nobel Prize winners. Sometimes, men who expect to undergo sterilization or chemotherapy also arrange to freeze and store a sample of their sperm. Preserved in a liquid nitrogen vat at minus 196 degrees centigrade (−320.8°F), sperm can be thawed and ready for use in a few minutes. Even five years after freezing it retains about sixty percent of its potency.

In 1978, in England, a human egg cell was fertilized in a petri dish. Baby Louise, the first genuine test tube baby, was the result. She was soon followed in many parts of the world, including the United States. In performing this feat, doctors first collect one egg from the mother's ovary, using instruments that allow them to look directly into her abdomen through two incisions—one in the navel and one close to the ovaries.

Next, the egg, now in a glass dish, rests in an incubator for a few hours. When a few drops of sperm cells are placed on the egg, fertilization takes place and cell division begins. As soon as the embryo has formed eight cells, it is ready to be implanted in the mother's womb through the cervix.

This procedure is followed when the mother is unable to conceive because her fallopian tubes are blocked or have been surgically removed. If, however, she is unable to go through any part of pregnancy but wishes to bring up her husband's child as her own, a surrogate, or host, mother may be found who will accept the husband's sperm in artificial insemination, then carry the baby to term and surrender it after birth.

A host mother may also be willing to accept the implant of a test tube–fertilized embryo by another couple, nurture it in her womb, and return it to its genetic parents when it is born.

Who is the real mother and who the real father in these cases? Usually, contracts are drawn up by lawyers before insemination takes place. Still, such novel means of bringing a child into the world are surrounded by emotional, ethical, and legal complications.

Religious groups that oppose abortion tend also to be against artificial insemination because they consider it adulterous and in other ways immoral. Not only that: in spite of contracts, law courts in some states may declare a child conceived by AID illegitimate or may pronounce the sperm donor to be the legal father. In one California case, a host mother refused to give up the child to its donor father and his wife, and was supported by the court in claiming the right to keep the baby. In fact, a transaction in which a woman is paid for becoming pregnant and producing a baby is always illegal because it violates the laws against child selling.

Objections and Controversy

Even within the medical community there is disagreement on these important issues. One of them concerns the entire concept of prenatal testing for birth defects. Some doctors believe that testing is not nearly widespread enough, while others emphasize that testing has its dangers and that its uses are limited.

Amniocentesis is usually administered only to expectant mothers in high-risk categories. This includes women over thirty-five, those who have had a previous abnormal birth, or those whose family (or husband's family) harbors a known chromosomal, biochemical, or open spinal cord disorder.

In 1977, though, a controlled study conducted in Denmark came up with startling results. Amniocentesis with chromosome analysis was performed on 1,806 pregnant women some of whom were considered high risk and others low risk. Chromosomal abnormalities were found to be about equally distributed among both groups.

Similarly, as we have seen, an American study of the incidence of Down's syndrome, or mongolism, reveals that it is not enough to screen only women over the age of thirty-five, since fathers and young mothers can also contribute to the disease.

Some opponents of testing stress the hazards of amniocentesis and other procedures that may disturb the baby in the womb. They believe that prenatal tests could very well pose a greater threat to the fetus than genetic defects. They also cite the possibility of errors in diagnosis, perhaps resulting in the abortion of a healthy infant. Finally, they stress the fact that no test can rule out every single one of thousands of possible birth disorders.

Again, however, this negative view is contradicted by a 1976 report from the National Institute of Child Health and Human Development. The Institute conducted a study of two groups of mothers, one who underwent amniocentesis in mid-trimester of pregnancy and one who did not. The two groups showed no significant difference in complications of pregnancy or delivery, number of miscarriages, or evidence of injury to the fetus, and the results of the diagnostic tests turned out to be 99.4 percent accurate.

Even so, the debate goes on, constantly fueled by new studies. One, by the University of California in San Francisco, found fourteen diagnostic errors in three thousand procedures, from which the group concluded that prenatal diagnosis is safe and highly accurate.

On the whole, critics have found flaws in the design of every study to date, either because the number of subjects was too small or because not enough controls were used.

Fear of Abuse
Can reproductive technology lead to abuse? Will women sell their eggs the way men now sell their sperm? Will women "rent out" their wombs as incubators? Can sperm donors be sued for child support? And how about parents who learn from a karyotype that their baby is normal but who decide to abort it because it isn't of the sex they wanted?

The medical profession tries to guard against abuses of this kind. For example, genetic laboratories of hospitals seldom accept patients for amniocentesis and karyotyping unless they are in a high-risk category. Besides, doctors do not disclose the sex of the fetus unless parents specifically request the information, in which case it cannot legally be kept from them.

As for other ethical issues that may arise, there are as yet no well defined laws to cover many of them, simply because they are brand-new problems. Certainly, the possibility of treating the unborn raises fresh moral dilemmas. Should a sick fetus be considered a patient in his or her own right? In that case it would be the doctor's sworn duty to try to keep the fetus alive, even against the wishes of the parents. Who would decide whether to treat or to abort a severely disabled unborn child? Can the law force mothers to undergo surgery or treatment for the embryo in the womb? If so, abortion might once more become illegal.

Traditionally, a fetus is considered a patient from the moment of birth, after physical separation from the mother. Today, however, when even a 1-pound (0.45-kg) baby may be kept alive by intensive care, this concept is changing. New medical techniques are giving different meaning to the nine-month dawn of human life.

6
The Frankenstein Question: Hazards and Ethics

A new discovery enabling humans to change basic life processes is bound to cause uneasiness and stir up controversy. No matter how promising it seemed, DNA recombination also had disturbing potential.

In July 1974, an unheard-of event occurred in the American scientific community. A group of ten scientists working mainly in microbiology issued a public letter to biologists everywhere, asking them to put a temporary stop to recombinant DNA research. A meeting would be called to assess the dangers of the new techniques and to safeguard the public.

THE QUESTION OF GENE SPLICING
Somewhat earlier in the 1970s two California researchers had taken a crucial step when they found a way to remove hereditary information from one organism and insert it into another. In this early gene-splicing experiment (the process is described in Chapter III), the scientists withdrew the genes conferring antibiotic resistance from two harmful bacteria: staphylococcus and salmonella. Using the techniques that have now become standard, they inserted these gene sections into the bacteria *E. coli*. Experiments are

often done using antibiotic-resistant strains because success or failure can be tested by exposing the final product to antibiotics. Some of the injected bacteria were found to have become antibiotic-resistant, proving that the foreign genes had been successfully transferred.

These antibiotic-resistant *E. coli* served no useful function. What was important about the experiment was that it demonstrated a procedure for recombining genetic material with simplicity and precision.

Once this was accomplished, it became evident that the technique was simple enough to permit some irresponsible person to combine the DNA of any two organisms and produce a "monster": a new disease-carrying, or cancer-causing, or antibiotic-resistant organism.

As in the story of Dr. Frankenstein, it seemed possible that the creation could turn on its creator and become destructive. By making it possible to bring forth new virulent life or large quantities of dangerous products, were biologists about to unleash plagues and incurable illnesses? Were they about to change the course of evolution?

One of the scientists who called for an international meeting to discuss biohazards was Paul Berg whose own research involved splicing DNA from SV40, a monkey tumor virus, into bacterial cells. By that time, however, he had abandoned certain parts of it as potentially hazardous. Dr. Berg received a 1980 Nobel Prize for his pioneering work.

The Asilomar Conference
The international meeting of concerned molecular biologists and biochemists took place in February 1975, at the Asilomar Conference Center in California. One of the first topics discussed was the bacterium *E. coli*, the microbial workhorse of the gene-splicing lab.

The particular strain of *E. coli* still used in research laboratories today was cultured in 1922 from the feces of a diphtheria patient. Over the years, the strain has become somewhat weakened. Scientists doubt that it could survive on its own outside the laboratory. Still, there were fears that *E. coli* programmed for antibiotic resistance or containing cancer-causing viral material, or producing hormones or toxins, might invade the intestinal tract of a laboratory worker and move from there to the general population.

Present at the conference were a number of experienced cancer virologists and microbiologists used to dealing with infectious organisms. Some of them did not think the new experiments unusually dangerous. They felt that as long as standard safety procedures were followed in laboratories, no further official restrictions were necessary. At one point in the conference, James Watson speculated that genetic engineering work was probably no more hazardous than working in a hospital.

The discussion brought out one important fact: participants in the conference had no way of knowing how dangerous their collective work might prove to be. The entire subject was so new and had developed so fast that data were not yet available. In spite of all these difficulties, the conferees reached consensus on a final document establishing three categories of risk for gene-splicing experiments and recommending safety procedures within each category. Moderate and high-risk experiments were to be done only with special strains of crippled or "disarmed" bacteria, unable to survive in natural surroundings.

These guidelines for academic research laboratories have essentially remained in effect. They were reformulated and made more specific by the National Institutes of Health's (NIH) Recombination Advisory Committee operating under pressure from Congress and the general public. On January 29, 1980, the guidelines were officially entered in the Federal Register.

Public Alarm
News media covering the Asilomar Conference were quick to tell the public that biologists were teaching old bugs new tricks. Even though scientists had convened and taken pro-

tective steps, people who had recently become aware of the dangers of nuclear power now angrily demanded safety from what seemed a new peril. Anxiety ran high in the neighborhood of several university biology labs. This was especially true in Cambridge and Boston where both Harvard and MIT (Massachusetts Institute of Technology) were already in the forefront of DNA research.

When it became clear that Harvard and MIT were upgrading labs to meet safety regulations and were ready to proceed with DNA experiments, the mayor called both universities to account. He asked for a moratorium, or period of delay, on further research and formed a citizens' committee to evaluate the situation.

A few stormy months followed. Many citizens were alarmed, while some of the scientists were surprised and irritated. They had tried to regulate their own work and instead of being praised they were attacked and virtually put on trial.

Eight months of testimony, debate, and mutual outrage ended with a settlement in favor of science. Recognizing the importance of freedom of inquiry and the possible benefits to humanity of DNA engineering, the city council voted to let research continue, provided National Institutes of Health safety regulations were strictly observed.

Easing Standards
In the years following Asilomar, molecular biologists have become more and more reluctant to be restricted in their research. The issue of biosafety has receded into the background. As the field has expanded and become familiar, workaday attitudes have replaced the former sense of awe. Projected accidents have not occurred. Researchers have not contracted "doomsday bugs," and no monsters have been created to escape.

Containment of dangerous organisms in genetics labs now seems to many experts mainly a matter of correct laboratory procedure, as practiced in other biological and medical facilities. Experience has shown that the weakened bacterial strains serving as vehicles for genetic transplants are indeed incapable of colonizing the human body.

In April 1981, a Federal Recombinant DNA Advisory Committee met to revise the old guidelines.

After eight months of study, the committee recommended relaxing regulations without making them entirely voluntary. It recommended giving more responsibility to bio-safety committees in local institutions. Today, about 95% of recombinant research—most of it using weakened bacteria or brewer's yeast—is practiced free of restrictions.

The committee also recommended a change of status in certain experiments that were formerly labeled "prohibited." Among these are experiments enabling harmless bacteria to make deadly toxins, and experiments making harmful bacteria resistant to drugs. Any such manipulation, as well as any deliberate move to release recombinant organisms into the environment, would still require prior review and approval by the National Institutes of Health.

Truth Seeking and Profit Making

Science often begins in free inquiry and ends in profit-making technology. Some observers regret this change from pure research to practical application; others welcome it. Popular opinion tends to hold that research of any kind is justified only if it turns up something useful. On the other hand, one must consider the earnest view of Erwin Chargaff, the renowned biochemist who laid some of the groundwork for the discovery of DNA structure. As he once told a group of college students, he prefers to think of science as a way to learn the truth about nature, not as a way to change it.

Some critical science-watchers fear that what looks to us now like a harvest of benefits to humanity, may end up doing more for large corporations than for people. A few giant business empires already control the production of such things as pharmaceutical drugs, chemicals, pesticides, cattle hormones, fertilizers, seeds, and grains. Genetic engineering holds out the promise of huge profits. This leaves little room for small business enterprises.

Other questions come to mind. Will corporate entities allow for competitive pricing? Will they conscientiously maintain genetic diversity of agricultural strains so that an unexpected pest or blight would not create disaster? Will they consider nutrition and taste in their products? Will giant companies protect the public from biohazards when they have yet to be careful about toxic wastes, air and water pollution, worker safety, and cancer-causing food additives?

Gloomy Prophecies

A few "worst case" prophecies by critics of genetic engineering come close to science fiction. They range from the possible development of biological warfare organisms that would selectively eliminate young people or members of one sex, to the advent of an ultimate doomsday bug to end all human life. They also raise the old specter of eugenics— human hereditary stock improvement—with all its abhorrent possibilities of abuse, and its threat of domination by one social or ethnic group over others.

ARE SCIENTISTS DISTURBING EVOLUTION?

Are scientists "playing God?" The question has been debated by religious leaders of every faith. Some find it arrogant to tamper with life as God created it. Other theologians point to the passage in the Bible where God tells Adam and Eve to "be fruitful and multiply and fill the earth and subdue it, and have dominion over . . . every living thing that moves upon the earth." To them, it seems that men and women were put in charge of nature, to use it and change it for their own benefit.

Robert Sinsheimer, a major figure in molecular biology, voices his concern in scientific terms. He believes that all experiments exchanging genes between bacteria (whose DNA is not confined within a nucleus) and higher organisms (whose DNA is confined within a nuclear membrane) are unpredictable and unsafe. He objects to scientists' tampering with the process of evolution, upsetting balances that have been set by the trial and error of millennia, and speeding up the pace of natural development. He draws attention to the fact that evolution has not crossed the barrier between animals and plants, nor between bacteria and more complex organisms—perhaps for good reasons which we do not understand. Finally, he thinks that humans are not yet wise enough to direct the course of their evolution.

On the other hand, some proponents of genetic engineering believe that gene transfer between bacteria and higher organisms is not a human invention at all but may, in fact, be going on all the time without our knowledge. As for disturbing evolution, humans began doing that long ago. Modern medicine, by saving young lives, continually interferes with evolutionary patterns. Even by the simple means of correcting our vision with eyeglasses, we change the evolutionary rule by which people who can't see well enough to hunt and gather food may be eliminated from the gene pool in early youth.

Finally, what some observers harshly call "playing God," seems to others no more than the fulfillment of a duty on the part of humans to guide their own destiny. In any case, an infinite distance yet lies between the laboratory creation of a mouse, which was recently accomplished, and the laboratory creation of a complete man or woman.

Genetic engineering reawakens the ancient dream of perfecting human beings and the life they lead on earth. But such a dream is far from simple to put into practice. Technical power must be used with respect and concern. Like all power, it can be used for good or ill. Its application lies in the hands of future generations.

Glossary

Amino acids. The chemical "building blocks" that are linked together to form proteins. The proteins of all species are made up from the same set of twenty different amino acids.

Amniocentesis. A medical procedure allowing doctors to examine the amniotic fluid that surrounds the unborn baby in the mother's womb.

Anticodon. The triplet of bases on the transfer RNA molecule that is complementary to the codon of messenger RNA.

Antigen. A foreign molecule that stimulates the production of specific antibodies.

Autosomal disorders. Genetic disorders in any of the twenty-two autosomes.

Autosomes. The twenty-two pairs of chromosomes that are identical in the cells of both sexes, as distinguished from the twenty-third pair, the sex chromosomes.

Bacteriophage. A virus that infects bacteria. It lives and multiplies inside the bacterium.

Bacterium. A microorganism, such as *E. coli*, with a cell wall and a chromosome not enclosed within a nucleus.

Bases. The set of chemical substances present in DNA and RNA: adenine, guanine, thymine, cytosine, and uracil. Their organization contains the genetic information.

Cell. A microscopic structure of plant or animal life, consisting of living matter within a membrane.

Cell fusion. A technique for combining two different cells.

Chimeric DNA. A combination of unrelated genes. The name comes from the mythic monster, the Chimera, which had a lion's head, goat's body, and serpent's tail.

Chromosomes. Threadlike structures in the cells. Chromosomes carry hereditary material in the form of genes.

Cleaving, Cleavage. A term applied to the cutting of DNA strands at specific sites by means of restriction enzymes.

Clone. One of a group of genetically identical cells all descended from a single common parent cell.

Codon. The sequence of three bases on DNA or RNA that codes for a particular amino acid.

Complementary bases. The exact pairing of bases that bind strands of nucleic acid together. In DNA, adenine always pairs with thymine, and guanine always pairs with cytosine; in RNA adenine always pairs with uracil.

Complementary DNA. A form of DNA synthesized from messenger RNA by means of the enzyme reverse transcriptase.

Conjugation. A bacterial mating process.

Cytology. The study of the structure and functions of cells.

Cytoplasm. The region of a cell outside the nucleus and within the membrane.

Diploid. Having a double set of chromosomes. Human cells (excepting the reproductive cells) are diploid, containing two sets of 23 chromosomes each. (Reproductive cells are haploid, containing only one set.)

DNA. The chemical compound DeoxyriboNucleic Acid which contains the hereditary information in a cell.

DNA ligase. An enzyme that helps in joining the two DNA strands that make up the double helix. Also aids in repairing damaged DNA.

DNA polymerase. One of the enzymes involved in DNA replication. It helps position the proper nucleotides onto the template and supply the energy to join them together to form a chain.

Double helix. The shape of the DNA molecule. The structural model of DNA, first conceived by Crick and Watson, consists of two long strands of DNA twisted about each other.

E. coli. A common type of bacteria found in the human intestines. It is generally considered harmless and is often used in gene splicing.

EcoR1. A restriction enzyme found in *E. coli,* used to cleave DNA at a unique site.

Embryo. An organism in the early stages of formation. The embryonic stage in humans extends through the first eight weeks in the womb.

Enzymes. Chemical substances that act to set off or speed up the chemical reactions in all biological systems.

Eukaryotes. A general name for organisms whose cells contain a nucleus and more than one chromosome.

Exons. The sequence of codons on the split-genes of higher organisms which codes for a particular protein. Exons are usually interrupted by a sequence of introns.

F factor. Fertility factor in "male" bacterial cells. It is responsible for the formation of a sex pilus.

Fetus. An unborn animal in the intermediate and late stages of formation. In humans the fetal stage lasts from the ninth week until birth.

Gene amplification. An increase in the amount of genetic material and number of individual genes on the chromosomes of a cell. It plays an important part in evolution and is also used by industry to step up bacterial output of proteins.

Gene mapping. Locating the positions of all the genes on the chromosomes of a particular organism.

Genes. Molecules of DNA (or, in certain organisms, RNA) that are carried on the chromosomes. Each gene carries the code for synthesis of a specific protein.

Genetic code. The relationship linking the sequence of bases in DNA or RNA to the sequence of amino acids in proteins.

Genome. The quantity of DNA that carries the complete set of genetic instructions for an organism.

Genotype and *phenotype.* Terms used to distinguish between the genetic constitution of an organism (genotype) and the observable constitution (phenotype).

Haploid. Refers to the number of chromosomes in germ cells. The human sperm and egg nuclei contain only twenty-three chromosomes each, or half the number of other human cells. They form a complete (diploid) set when they combine.

Heterozygous. Carrying an unmatched gene for any particular autosomal hereditary trait (except for X-linked traits).

Homologous recombination. The exchange of segments of DNA between chromosomal regions during meiosis.

Homozygous. Carrying genes for any particular hereditary trait on each of two chromosomes.

Hybrid. Offspring of genetically diverse parents.

Hydrogen bond. A weak chemical bond resulting from the uneven distribution of electrons about certain atoms, that links hydrogen to such atoms as oxygen and nitrogen. It is one of the most important weak interactions between biological molecules.

Introns. Segments of noncoding "nonsense" bases that interrupt the coding sequences of bases carrying the hereditary message in the split genes of higher organisms. The role played by introns is still unknown.

In vitro. The term literally means "in glassware." *In vitro* experiments are distinguished from those performed directly on animals or humans, (*in vivo*).

Karyotype. The organized chart of the chromosomes of a cell. A karyotype is made for the purpose of counting and examination of chromosomes.

Lambda phage. An example of a bacterial virus that has two different life cycles. After infecting the bacterium it can multiply in the usual manner and destroy its host. Under certain conditions, however, it can become integrated with the chromosomes of the host bacterium and remain dormant.

Lyse. To cause cells to dissolve or burst. The process is called lysis.

Meiosis. The process by which the human reproductive cells (germ cells) are formed. In meiosis the cell divides twice, but the chromosomes duplicate only once. As a result, the male and female germ cells are haploid, which means that they contain half the usual number of chromosomes, twenty-three instead of forty-six.

Messenger RNA. The intermediate RNA molecule that is synthesized in the cell nucleus according to instructions encoded in DNA. It then moves out into the body of the cell carrying its "message" to the ribosomes, where the proteins are made.

Microorganisms. General term for microscopic plant or animal life.

Mitochondria. Tiny capsule-shaped bodies found in all cells. They contain enzymes that aid in the release of energy from food. Frequently called the "powerhouses" of cells.

Mitosis. The process by which cells divide and multiply.

Molecular biology. The study of the molecular structure and chemical reactions of living cells.

Molecule. The smallest subunit of a compound consisting of two or more atoms.

Monoclonal antibodies. Genetically engineered hybrid cells that are cloned and cultured to produce pure, specific antibodies.

Mutation. A change in the genes caused by alteration in the structure of its DNA or RNA.

Nucleotide. A chemical compound that consists of a base, a sugar, and one or more phosphate groups. The basic structural unit of DNA and RNA.

Organism. Any form of life having one or more cells, including bacteria, plants, and humans.

Peptide bond. The chemical bond linking the amino acids in proteins.

Phage. See Bacteriophage.

Phenotype. See Genotype and phenotype.

Plasmids. Small circular DNA molecules present in bacteria that are accessory to a bacteria's chromosome. They reproduce independently and enable bacteria to transfer genetic material to each other.

Polygenic diseases. Hereditary disorders caused by defects in several genes.

Polynucleotide. A molecule composed of many nucleotide units linked to each other.

Prokaryotes. Those organisms whose cells have no nuclear membrane and only one chromosome.

Proteins. One of the most important groups of biological molecules. Enzymes, muscles, and connective tissue are all proteins. All proteins are constructed from combinations of the same set of twenty amino acids.

Protoplast. Bacterial cell whose outer cell wall has been removed.

Protoplast fusion. Procedure for forming a hybrid bacterial cell from two unrelated parent cells by removing the cell walls, fusing the two resultant protoplasts, and letting the cell wall regenerate.

Recombinant DNA. The creation of a new DNA molecule by the process of cleaving and rejoining different DNA strands.

Replication. The process whereby DNA reproduces itself.

Restriction enzyme. An enzyme that recognizes a specific base sequence in DNA, and cuts, or cleaves, the DNA chain at a specific site within the sequence.

Reverse transcriptase. An enzyme found in certain viruses that has the ability to reverse the usual DNA-to-RNA flow of information. The enzyme stimulates the synthesis of DNA from an RNA template.

R factor. R factor (resistance factor) plasmids, found in many microorganisms, contain r-genes that confer antibiotic resistance.

R-genes. The genes found in bacterial plasmids that confer resistance to certain drugs and antibiotics.

Ribosomal RNA. A form of RNA that is the major component of ribosomes. Its role in protein synthesis is still not known.

Ribosome. A complex structure found in cells that acts as the site for protein synthesis. It is made up of proteins and ribosomal RNA.

RNA. Ribonucleic acid (RNA) is a close chemical relative of DNA. It is usually a single-stranded molecule that differs from DNA in using the sugar ribose in its nucleotide backbone, and in substituting the base uracil for thymine.

Sex chromosomes. The chromosomes which determine gender. In humans, females have two X chromosomes (XX). Males have an X and a Y chromosome (XY).

Spina bifida. Defect in which the neural tube containing the spinal cord has failed to close. Also known as "open spine."

Split genes. Genes of higher organisms where the coded sequences of bases are interrupted by noncoding "nonsense" sequences of bases. The function of these discontinuities in the genetic information carried by the gene is not known.

Sticky ends. The ends of a DNA molecule that has been cleaved by a restriction enzyme. These ends are called sticky because they combine with, or stick to, a complementary sequence of bases on another DNA strand.

SV 40. A virus that induces tumors in monkeys.

Synthesis. The making of a complex chemical substance by combining simpler compounds or elements.

Terminal transferase. An enzyme that adds a tail, consisting of a predetermined sequence of nucleotides, to the end of one of the strands of a DNA molecule.

Transcription. The process by which the genetic information in DNA is copied to form messenger RNA (mRNA) molecules.

Transfer RNA. A form of RNA that is coded to collect the amino acids needed for protein synthesis and "transfer" them to their proper position on messenger RNA at the ribosomes. There is at least one transfer RNA molecule for each kind of amino acid.

Transformation. A process of introducing foreign DNA, such as plasmids, into a bacterial cell.

Translation. The process by means of which the genetic message carried by messenger RNA assembles a protein molecule in the ribosome.

Vector. A vehicle for moving DNA from one cell to another, such as a plasmid into which foreign DNA can easily be inserted and which will be efficiently taken up by the host cell.

Virus. A disease-causing agent that consists of a core of DNA or RNA enclosed in a protective coat. Viruses reproduce only in living cells.

X-linked. The term is used to speak of genetic traits or diseases located on the X or sex chromosomes.

X-ray diffraction. The technique of determining the structure of molecules using the visible patterns obtained by the scattering of X rays from crystals.

Recommended Books

Frankel, Edward. *DNA: The Ladder of Life*. New York: McGraw Hill, 1979.

Genetic Engineering, Human Genetics, and Cell Biology. Committee on Science and Technology, U.S. House of Representatives. U.S. Government Printing Office, 1980.

Harsanyi, Zsolt, and Richard Hutton. *Genetic Prophecy: Beyond the Double Helix*. New York: Wade, 1981.

Impact of Applied Genetics: Micro-Organisms, Plants, and Animals. Office of Technology Assessment. U.S. Government Printing Office, undated.

"Industrial Microbiology." *Scientific American*. September, 1981.

Judson, Horace Freeland. *The Eighth Day of Creation*. New York: Simon and Schuster, 1979.

Lygre, David G. *Life Manipulation: From Test-Tube Babies to Aging*. New York: Walker, 1979.

Recombinant DNA: Readings from Scientific American. San Francisco: W. H. Freeman, 1978.

Wade, Nicholas. *The Ultimate Experiment*. New York: Walker, 1977.

Watson, James. *The Double Helix*. New York: Atheneum, 1968. (An important classic.)

Watson, James, and John Tooze. *The DNA Story*. San Francisco: W. H. Freeman, 1981.

Index